Blur

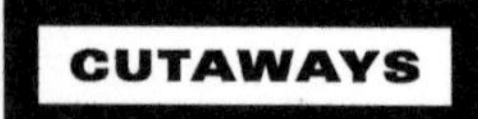

"This new series of small-format books focused on cinematic motifs, themes, and devices represents something new and exciting in English-language writing on film." —**Dennis Lim, Artistic Director, New York Film Festival**

"Featuring some of the field's most exciting scholars and critics, Cutaways is a welcome addition to film writing. The series promises to expand the ways cinema is conceived, consumed, and received, in ways that parallel the contemporary situation of cinema." —**Sarah Keller, author of *Anxious Cinephilia: Pleasure and Peril at the Movies***

Cutaways is a series of pocket-sized books by and for movie lovers. Each volume offers a journey through the history of cinema guided by a single motif or formal device. Featuring original writing by film scholars and critics, the books create a space for intellectually engaged and broadly accessible cinephilia.

Blur

Martine Beugnet
Translated by Lindsay Turner

FORDHAM UNIVERSITY PRESS   NEW YORK   2026

This book was first published in French as *L'attrait du flou*, by Martine Beugnet © Yellow Now, 2017.

Fordham University Press gratefully acknowledges financial assistance and support provided for the publication of this book by ECHELLES UMR 8264 and AnimAtrium.

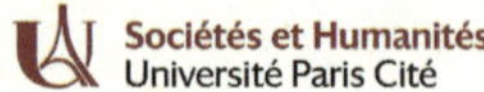

cnrs

Visit us online at www.fordhampress.com.

For EU safety / GPSR concerns: Mare Nostrum Group B.V., Mauritskade 21D, 1091 GC Amsterdam, The Netherlands, gpsr@mare-nostrum.co.uk

Library of Congress Cataloging-in-Publication Data available online at https://catalog.loc.gov.

Printed in the United States of America
28 27 26   5 4 3 2 1
First edition

Contents

Blur

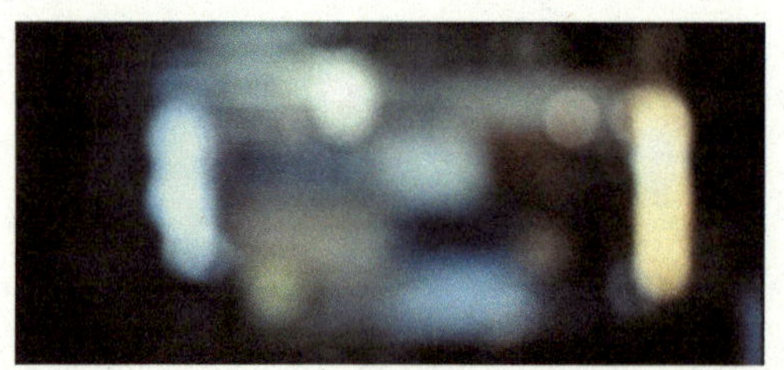

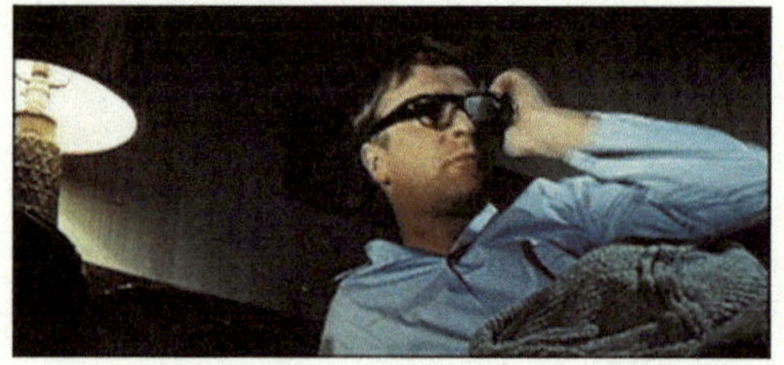

Prologue
Myopia

Yet we envy the short-sighted—that restless melancholy, that indistinct sight that gives rise to a certain sad sweetness, a tenderness . . .

—Dominique Chateau

Imagine an eye unruled by man-made laws of perspective, an eye unprejudiced by compositional logic, an eye which does not respond to the name of everything but which must know each object encountered in life through an adventure of perception.

—Stan Brakhage

I have astigmatism. Without my corrective lenses, my view of the world around me is blurry, double, and imprecise. Going to the movies without glasses is out of the question. But my interest in blur in film—in the hazy beauty of its apparitions, in nebulous outlines and indistinct shimmering backgrounds—does not arise from my defective vision. Instead, it comes from the fact that blur is meaningful on its own. All the same, I do have a weakness for nearsighted characters—and since the fate reserved for women who wear glasses is, on screen, rarely enviable, let's begin with a male character: Harry Palmer, the spy with the tortoiseshell glasses.[1]

Close-up of a half-open eye. There's a shrill ringing, irritating and interminable. Rapid zoom out: in the shadows, a man's face, half-asleep. He holds out a hand and the camera follows his movement; he turns on a light. Abrupt change of scale, low angle: The next shots make us feel the character's disorientation. Half-asleep, he fumbles with the sheets, sits up sharply, and looks around him confusedly. In place of a reverse shot that would help situate things, the pan we get instead is completely blurred: Spots of bluish color, rays and dots of light spread in bright lines and geometric forms. The shot resembles an abstract painting or a misty glimpse of an urban landscape seen through a window on a rainy night. The sequence lasts several brief seconds only. The man leans over toward the night table, finds his glasses, and puts them on. A new pan begins, but the brief moment of enchantment is gone: The mysterious blurry upsurge has been replaced by a clear vision of a cramped and ordinary interior.

Filmed in 1964, *The Ipcress File* (Sidney J. Furie) was released the same year as the fourth James Bond film (*Thunderball*, Terrence Young, 1965). But from the first frames on, it is clear that *The Ipcress File* is the antithesis of a 007-style spy film. Cynical and unfailingly caustic, Harry is also extremely myopic. The viewer, introduced to the character via the experience of blurry vision, is thus aware from the film's outset of the weakness, as well as perhaps the gentleness, that belies the sardonic attitude and apparent coldness of his blue eyes. His physical deficiency also points to what gives him his strength: Harry Palmer, the nearsighted spy, is rarely deceived by appearances.

From the close-up of the glowing light bulb to the mark left by the diaphragm in the blurred shot's glowing geometric forms, *The Ipcress File* highlights the cinematic techniques behind its making, revealing a singular formal ambition.[2] CinemaScope framing, depth of field, rack focus, perspectival distortion: Both the character's nearsightedness and his initial sleepiness are integrated into the film's baroque sensibility.

In the rest of the sequence, objects tend to occupy the foreground while the human figure is relegated to the background, out of the area of sharpest focus. Moreover, the long shot depicting the whole room, with Harry getting out of bed, is dominated by the visual and sonic presence of the alarm clock, the precise outline of which dominates the foreground. As the character wearily opens the curtains, his silhouette is backlit and caught in the blurry, fuzzed background. By an effect of synesthetic transfer, blurred vision here evokes a general dullness of all the senses—the uncertain space between sleep and waking.

It is no accident that credits and opening sequences often employ blur. Beyond the curiosity aroused by images that are not immediately "legible," blur creates a kind of buffer zone between the reality the spectator leaves when they enter the movie theater and the fictional world into which they are invited to be immersed. The blurriness that in this case shows Harry's progressive awakening—a process complicated by his myopia—also invites the viewer to put their awareness of the surrounding reality to sleep, and so to be more awake to the reality of the film.

In moments dominated by blur, the image resists the frame's signifying force—how, when the visual field is blurred, to select which portion of it has more or less meaning?—and the plot slips a little. In *The Ipcress File*, it is through the use of objects, standing in for the mechanics of cinema, that the conditions necessary for setting the plot in motion are established: The alarm clock sounds as a sort of call to clarity and sharpness, spurring our protagonist into action; as substitutes for the lens and frame, the large, rectangular pair of glasses prefigures the shift to focus that relegates blur to the margins of the visual field.

In narrative cinema, myopic or drugged vision is often the vehicle for ventures into the uncertain territory of blurriness, putting the temporarily indecipherable image to use for its humorous or anxiety-producing effects. But the completely blurred pan that appears at the beginning of *The Ipcress File* has a particular appeal, beyond serving as a transitional space or standing as a play on the subjective point of view of the nearsighted character. The sudden and—at this point—unexplained intrusion of blur appeals also because for an instant the eye is carried far from the normative universe of genre film. These brief images, unexpectedly "aris[ing] directly from the film's materials" to suspend its narrative and figurative thread at its very start, demonstrate the disruptive power of blur.[3] So blurry that it almost resembles a tachist painting, the shot creates a fleeting opening toward other types of images—practices at the intersection of cinema and painting, chance and intention—that have nothing a priori to do with classical narrative cinema.

This conjunction of the universes of genre film and experimental form is unusual—but then is it not precisely the function of blur to confuse borders, creating shadowy zones that confound both vision and judgment?

In Praise of Indistinction

The first quality of blur in mainstream cinema is to go unnoticed. The grammar of classical narrative cinema does include certain effects of blurriness, but force of habit has rendered these almost invisible. Whether it serves as punctuation (dissolves, the occasional quick pan) or is part of the frame's internal organization, blur remains at the margins of the "useful areas" toward which shifts or pull-focus transitions guide the gaze. (André Bazin deplored this pragmatic use of blur as a corollary to montage, which he viewed as anathema to the spectator's freedom of interpretation.[1])

Blur is also conventionally used to reproduce certain points of view (the myopic or sleepy gaze, or vision flooded by tears), represent particular atmospheric conditions (mist, fog, distant horizons), or suggest speed. With the aim of conveying "authenticity," a passage of amateur film shot on 8mm or a sequence caught with a cell phone or surveillance camera is sometimes integrated into a fictional story. Taken from elsewhere or created from scratch, this footage is recognizable by its clumsy, blurred rendering and by the deterioration or weak definition of its images. These conventional effects aside, however, blur is not supposed to be consciously perceived by the viewer: Except in the case of a freeze-frame, we often fail even to register a blurred background, no matter how magnificent.

If traditional narrative cinema tends to avoid conspicuous blur, this is because an unexpectedly blurry image draws attention to the workings of the camera; it risks undoing the illusion of reality. Blur returns film to what it has least mastered: the incessant, vertiginous movement that animates the tiniest particle of what it tries to capture; the slippage, during the shot's duration, of the figure ("contoured," immediately identifiable) toward its formless other; the fragility of the border separating the human form from a mere smudge.

Fans of blur might take a perverse pleasure in pointing out the optical skid that is buried, albeit fleetingly, at the heart of some of Hollywood's classic genre films. The aspect of contingency that enters every act of photochemical filmmaking is an important ally to blur.

For example: We find a prettily perturbing instance of accidental blur in the famous opening sequence of the musical comedy *Gold Diggers of 1933* (Mervyn LeRoy, 1933). The film begins with a medium shot of Ginger Rogers, cloaked in coins, singing "We're in the Money." A careful sequence of tight shots of the group of chorus girls who surround the singer offers us a veritable sampler of feminine figures, different yet basically interchangeable, before ending with a return to the initial framing of Rogers. While the camera approaches the actress in a slow forward tracking shot (zoom did not yet exist), a double disjunction occurs, sonic then visual. First, Rogers's words become difficult to understand: She switches from English into Pig Latin. And second, although the shot's forward tracking is still fluid, optics do not quite follow. The lens fails to focus; for several seconds while the actress's face fills the frame, her features soften and then blur.[2]

This irruption of blur is even more striking because it occurs as part of a rigorous mise-en-scène in which the filmed spectacle evokes a form of Taylorism (not without irony, since this ballet to the glory of the dollar takes place against the backdrop of economic crisis). Blur has no place in Busby Berkeley's choreography, the spectacular impact of which depends on the precise clockwork of the dancers' movements. The disarray—the blur of dispersal—that might be caused by the proliferation of bodies in the shot is checked by the perfect synchronization of their gestures and the geometric regularity of their configurations. Usually, framing, camera movements, and focus would all invisibly work together as bearers of this exacting spirit. But here, at the moment of the close-up, technique falters.

In a way, the focus error that occurs in the tracking shot arrives right on time, since it punctuates verbal disarray with a brief instant of visual chaos; as the actress's face comes into and out of focus, her vocal rhythm accelerates and the song's syllables garble. *Gold Diggers of 1933* was released at the end of a period of transition between silent film and talking pictures—it is the typical product of the technical evolution that aims to eliminate blur from the cinematographic image.

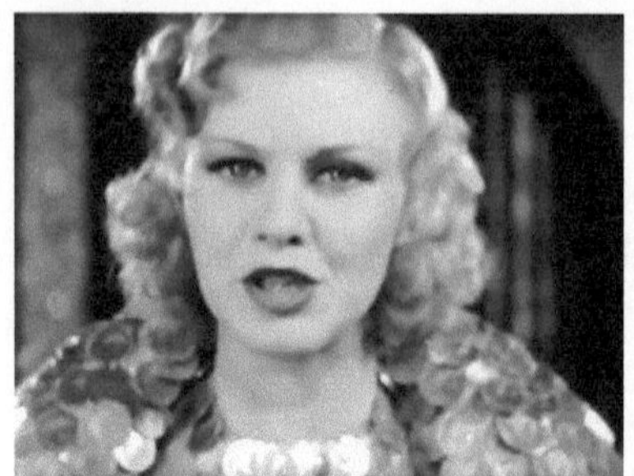 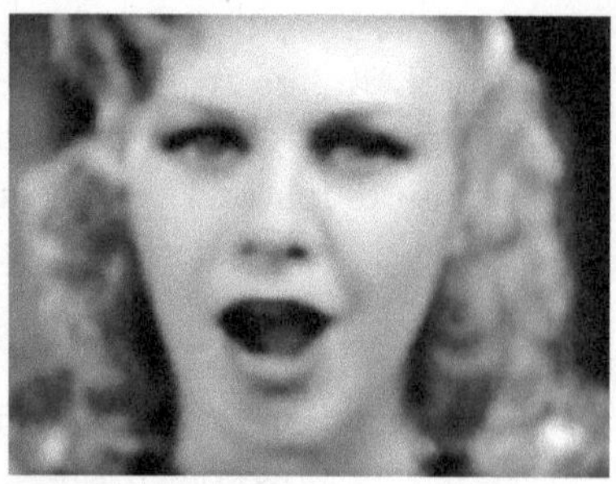

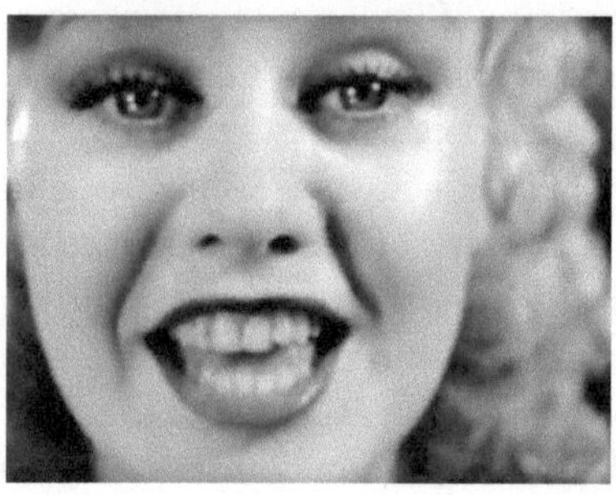

In order to be distinctly heard and localized in space, sounds must be precisely associated with bodily gestures and placement, and dialogue synchronized with lip movements: The close-ups of the singer's mouth lend themselves to representing verbal acrobatics, a powerful demonstration of the appeal of synchronized image and sound. All of this assumes the figure's carefully defined consistency. Yet however coincidentally, the temporary slippage toward blur allows the human shape to be seen in a different light: as an unstable entity, in a state of becoming, susceptible to the attraction of formlessness.

After it comes back into focus, the spectacle of Rogers's face in extreme close-up borders on the grotesque. Each detail is visible, from the cavernous mouth to the folds of the wrinkles, from teeth to lashes, precisely captured and monstrously enlarged. Have we now left behind those earlier silent-cinema faces, haloed in light, with their blurred contours and softened features? If this sharp close-up seems closer to faces filmed with a high-definition digital camera (we might think of the devastating close-ups of faces in Lars von Trier's *Melancholia*, 2011) than to the idealized faces of cinema's early days, this is because the quest for precision that dominates cinematic aesthetics after the arrival of the talkies is not limited to the mandatory synchronization of sound and image. Rather, it is part of a larger culture of sharpness, a desire to pin down the image and to penetrate its mysteries. This bent might be best described with the aid of a counterexample, a different introductory sequence that focuses on a group of young women but that this time takes the form of a radiant praise of vagueness.

The antithesis of the opening of *Gold Diggers* could be the beginning of *The Captive* (2000), Chantal Akerman's loose adaptation of Marcel Proust. Here too, the film starts with a group portrait—in this case, a beach scene inspired by Proust's *In the Shadow of Young Girls in Flower*. But as opposed to the ordered compositions and careful assortment of female figures offered by the musical, this collective portrait is composed instead as a eulogy to elusiveness, highlighting the softness specific to the 8mm image. In addition to possessing its own particular visual qualities, 8mm is the format of amateur film. Silent, with a slightly fluttering pace of projection, it is especially suited to evoking the feeling of unsteady evanescence that we associate with the earliest cinematic images, as well as the uncertainty of memory.

The noise of the projector. A group of young girls on the seaside. The grain of the image is marked and uneven. The delineation of the contours is faint: Bodies, sand, and waves are all held in the same crystalline glaze. Light and color are diffuse and delicate: Such seascape images, shot in 8mm film, are as close as cinema gets to watercolor—here we might recall, too, that one of the techniques of watercolor consists of sprinkling a wash with grains of salt. Blues dominate, set off by the beige of the sand and the pink and red of bathing suits. The unsteadiness created by the image's visible grain and the camera movement is further emphasized by the slight pulsation that occurs as the film passes through the projector.

Shot with a handheld camera, the bathing girls form a tight group. They are a little blurry; the camera seems to have trouble following them, and shots and framing are shaky. When the group is finally stilled, posing before the lens, the camera frames the faces in closer and closer shots before coming to rest on Ariane, the future captive of the title. Skin and film, the image's grain and Ariane's freckles: What we see becomes as soft and granular as a pointillist painting, where dots run into one another like so many infinitesimal circles of confusion.[3]

The next shot is in 35mm. Although dark, it is perfectly crisp, and it sets the 8mm images within it for the rest of the film. The images we have just seen are being watched by a man, alone, who keeps stopping and starting the projector. The same few frames—a medium shot of Ariane and her girlfriend Andrée facing the camera—are repeated. The man's voice joins the noise of the projector. Like someone dubbing a silent film, he tries to fit words to the movements of the young women's lips.[4] Then he approaches the screen, peering in close. But the blurry images resist the gaze that seeks to penetrate their secrets and the words that would fix them into one meaning. In the end, the man lets the reel go, and Ariane takes off toward the waves, the shape of her body becoming more and more indistinct as she distances herself from the camera.

Recent memory? Posthumous images? The temporality of 8mm film is as imprecise as the contours it renders; seen in retrospect, the beginning of *The Captive* seems in fact to follow the film's conclusion, in which Ariane, like the siren rejoining her sisters, ultimately escapes for good, disappearing into the sea.[5]

The existence of blur at the heart of the cinematic image preserves the presence of the unknown within it, whereas high definition and new technologies and viewing practices offer the "user" the possibility of revealing every secret. Such technologies, anticipated by *The Captive*'s projectionist when he halts the progression of the film to examine a freeze-frame, are always undermined by cinematic blur. Whether in the progressively blurrier photographic enlargements in Michelangelo Antonioni's *Blow-Up* (1966) or in the visual and sonic recordings by the surveillance expert in *The Conversation* (Francis Ford Coppola, 1974), dialogue is diluted by parasitic noise, and the image eventually dissolves, taking our sense of certainty with it. Blur, which appears in the very grain of 8mm footage, is part of every filmic image, analog or digital.

Neither the effects of blow-up—plunging the eye into the material—nor the freeze-frame, which suspends all movement, can overcome it. On the contrary: They reveal its hidden presence.

For *The Captive*'s jealous and possessive lover, the irreducibility of mystery is intolerable; destroying his love, the desire to know everything renders him insensible to the beauties of the blurred image.[6] As Daniel Arasse points out in his work on Vermeer, this sort of image works "not to make its object known but to make the viewer witness to a presence." What comes to be seen is therefore not "the secret of an observed nature" but indeed "a mystery inside the image itself, inside the visibility of its figures."[7]

Before the scene on the beach, the ocean was already present as the background for *The Captive*'s opening sequence, a shot of foamy breakers crashing loudly on the sand at night. Blur on blur: A blurred focus makes the 35mm look hazy. As the image sharpens, there still remains the spectacle of the natural confusion created by the movement and sound of the waves. In the shift to 8mm film that follows the credits, the noise of the projector replaces the noise of the sea, and the sound of the whirring film replaces the crashing of the waves.

Wave, in French, is *la vague*: Etymologies vary, but the meaning of words and the phenomena they describe intersect here.[8] The adjective "vague" comes from the Latin *vagus*: wandering, moving, undefined, indistinct. The origins of the noun are Indo-European but can also be traced back to the idea of incessant movement, to the permanent flux of the liquid element. Between form and formlessness, *la vague* remains elusive and can only be grasped imprecisely;[9] it is the very manifestation of perpetual motion and, as such, a privileged inspiration for poetic creation.[10] The wave pattern was also important for Leibniz, who saw it as the perfect example of clear versus obscure knowledge: We hear and can recognize "the noise of each wave" but without being able to discern its exact composition or separate it from the "roar" of the ocean.[11] Knowledge that comes from the senses, in other words, touches on the infinite universe of things and the relations between them. Lacking the properties of "clarity and distinction" that are proper to scientific knowledge, sensory knowledge is necessarily and inextricably imprecise. It is thus from the sensory that the aesthetic arises—the pursuit and the expression of the je ne sais quoi that moves us, that art strives to capture and to cultivate, and that we feel, as at the sight of the high sea with its crashing waves, without being able to perceive or explain exactly what constitutes it.

Incessant movement, intermingling of parts into the whole: The indistinct—the wave, the vague—is at the heart of cinema, whether in the case of the blurring together of its twenty-four projected images per second or in the camera's capture of the real. By their nature, because the camera's mechanical eye records all that it can represent, cinematic images excel at depicting what refuses to be fixed—what the human eye tends not consciously to register. This propensity to capture everything, however, does not make cinema into a tool of scientific knowledge. Quite the contrary.[12] As the excitement of the first moviegoers reminds us, what cinema reveals is confusion. Having attended the 1896 projections of short films by the Lumière brothers, *Repas de bébé* (1895), *L'arrivée d'un train* (1896), and *La baignade en mer* (1895), the journalist Henri de Parville marveled at being able to make out "all the details, the windmills of smoke that arose, the waves of the sea as they broke upon the beach, the trembling of leaves caught in the breeze."[13] Whether it affects a part or the whole of the image, blur does not signal some lack. On the contrary, it shows an excess of detail, an intensification and a dispersion of movement that the human eye also captures, in reality, unconsciously or indistinctly. Jean Epstein, filmmaker of storms, never ceased to affirm this principle in his writings and films: It is the role of the art of cinema to develop an aesthetic that cultivates a primary inclination toward the contingent, the undefined, and the unstable. Because it renders the confused exuberance of the real as captured on film, blur [*flou*] also helps eliminate the superfluous [*superflu*], pulling film toward the painterly.

In so many ways, the filmic image is predisposed toward blur. Captured and perceived in time, subject to the variations of light and movement, it is also prey to a variety of optical and chemical metamorphoses that endlessly reproduce the palette of the vague, the misty, the fleeting.

Today more than ever, however, the aesthetic of the moving image privileges the qualities of mastery, stabilization, and instant recognition. Figures have clean lines, faces have immediately identifiable features, dialogue is perfectly synchronized.

How to explain the prevalence of the view that the moving image is destined for ever-increasing definition and resolution? In large part, this fact stems from an obsession with communication, as well as the way we imagine technological evolution. In this model of thinking, the visual serves as a metaphor for the conceptual, and progress itself means progress toward the "clear and distinct." Cinema, after all, was born out of a machine. It is the product of an industrial and technological modernity whose advent caused what Jean-Louis Comolli described as a "frenzy of the visible."[14] Developments in optics and media formats, increased sensitivity of film stock and lens precision, and the possibilities of post-production correction: All of these are part of the conflation of progress and the increased legibility of the visible field. Begun with the first experiments with high-speed photography (Eadweard Muybridge is sometimes described as the precursor of the "bullet time" effect), this conflation prevails today in the discourse around very-high-definition digital images. And indeed, we continue to use the phrase "fuzzy logic" to describe modes of reasoning that fall outside of strictly established categories.[15] Blur remains commonly considered, above all, as a *lack* of clearness—the sign of a deficiency.

Yet we know that indeterminacy and incompleteness are essential parts of the spectator's experience—that even a few damp spots on a wall can sustain the desire to imagine and to project better than a minutely detailed image.[16] "The value of an image is measured by the extent of its *imaginary* aura," writes Gaston Bachelard. "This amounts to saying that a stable and completed image *clips the wings of imagination*."[17]

The development of sfumato, a major innovation of Leonardo da Vinci's work, corresponded to precisely this need to reconcile an abstract conception of representation with perception, to accommodate the "actual" outlines of bodies to the forms of their "visibility." Shading is used to account for the imprecision of the contours of figures seen up close or far away.[18] For cinema, however, the inaccessible and sterile ideal of the perfectly defined image recalls the uncertainties of the early days, the specter of the soulless copy and the Baudelairean affirmation of the impossible alliance of art and photography. The history of cinema as art was established in opposition to this axiom. In this history, blur plays a key role: From the first film avant-gardes onward, the refusal of the normative image and resistance to the ideal of mimetic precision involves blur.

While the introduction of sound certainly condemned the filmic image to a surfeit of clarity, it did not end the debate over the qualities of the image itself. In the 1940s, visual style founded on maximal depth of field was criticized for the hardness of its contours and its lack of volume.[19] And if today the digital aesthetic is not universally preferred, this is often because it tends toward excess definition. From the flat, dull look typical of the images created by the first automatic digital cameras' small sensors (which captured things indiscriminately, from foreground to background) to experiments in high-speed shooting and projection (the HFR, or "high frame rate," used by Peter Jackson for *The Hobbit*, 2012) that produce images resembling a badly designed video game, many uses of digital video until now have proved unconvincing. Isn't it in the instability of outlines, however barely perceptible, that the trembling of life leaves its trace in the filmic image?

Blur's Paradox: Images That Kill

And yet, paradoxically, blur—the guarantor of the image's mystery, of its lifelike pulsation—also proves to be a useful prop to deathly discourses of mastery and to the justification of the unjustifiable. Nowhere more acutely than in war footage can this paradox be felt. Describing the parallel development of cinematic and military technologies and the key function of aerial shots in both fields, Paul Virilio points out the correlation of the lens's field of vision with that of the shooting field.[20] Military images are often described as "operational" or "operative" images, that is, as images produced not for artistic, documentary, or entertainment purposes but as practical tools used for monitoring, detection, identification, and tracking purposes.[21] Accordingly, in the conflation of the camera's lens and the weapon's target finder, some of the war footage originating from the battlefield effectively contains "images that kill."[22] At the same time, much of the aerial footage that we see as part of the official and nonofficial accounts of operations in conflict zones offers little legibility to the unschooled eye: Distant drone and helicopter footage tends to be blurred and shaky, with the scale of things difficult to assess. In the absence of translation into a readily understandable visual form or of an expert reading and interpretation, to the average observer this footage often remains partly or wholly meaningless.[23] The poor, blurry, or schematic image captured from afar is thus both a hindrance and a necessity. It does not merely grant authority to a specialist discourse but contributes to the operative setup itself: The sense of remoteness and estrangement is part and parcel of augmented vision's transformation of the body of the other into a target.

Éléonore Weber's *Il n'y aura plus de nuit* (2020) is a found-footage film through and through, solely composed of operational images.[24] It consists of a montage of sequences shot and posted by military pilots. The selected footage was filmed from American and French helicopters flying over conflict zones in the Middle East, namely, Iraq, Syria, and Afghanistan, with a preeminence of infrared footage. The voiceover explains how the heightened sensitivity of the camera to light and heat accounts for the otherworldly quality of the nocturnal images. With their fluctuating spectrum of scintillation and translucence and blurry outlines, the sequences often display an exquisite sense of eeriness. At the same time, the rough surface of some of the aerial shots of mountainous reliefs resembles an extreme close-up of skin. The uncertainty generated by the confrontation with such operational images is ceaselessly evoked in the observations of the gunner who agreed to watch and comment on Weber's chosen footage and complains that he sees too much or not enough. The tiny, trembling monochrome silhouettes and scintillating bodies that appear on our screens have the spectral, unreal appearance of the humanoid targets that populate obsolete video games. The repercussions are, in the face of such doubt, terrifying: To watch sequences that include the annihilation of "targets" is to witness lethal destruction that is triggered by the most tenuous of clues. Just as certain forms of discourse, when confronted with the experience of not knowing, define their own object, here the viewfinder, as it superimposes itself on the visible, labels the target, no matter how indefinite the image of its shape.

High-Definition Blur

Although intuitively we associate blur with low-definition and the "poor" image, high definition does not necessarily entail its disappearance.[25] It is possible to film blurry things in high definition. They can be entirely fabricated, depth of field can be reduced, or the image can be blurred in post-production. HD or not, shapes filmed through fog retain an undefined aspect on screen. Certainly, the quality of fog filmed in high definition, rendered with maximum resolution, is unique to the digital image; it would appear as a spread of fine particles, a sort of pointillism, rather than as a vaporous and enveloping layer, as it would on analog film. But digital technology adapts, seeking to emulate the irregular softness of analog images (the aleatory reaction of salt crystals on the surface of celluloid film) and the graininess of certain film formats. In effect, contemporary optical technologies allow for sumptuously blurred effects.

But these technologies also give rise to an increase in visual clichés. Among the motifs that fill the green screens of films employing digital special effects, blur no longer suggests uncertainty and mystery but is now instead a sign, one denotative element among others in a conventional system of forms and meanings. Harry Potter has only to recognize an evil spirit in a studio cemetery in order to set an entire assortment of digital effects into motion: a whole panoply of fogs, mists, clouds, double exposures, transparencies, dissolutions, and various vaporous emanations. If in all of this we can recognize the pleasures associated with the spectacle of B-movie kitsch bricolage in the vein of Ed Wood, updated to contemporary tastes by computer-generated imagery and digital post-production, we are still far removed from the unsettling visual disorder that blur creates through other filmmaking practices.

Moreover, commercial cinema, music videos, and advertising all tend to use (and abuse) a palette of normative effects, among which blur generally serves as an artistic alibi: See, for example, the proliferation of textured backdrops and other *bokeh* effects, thanks to which the individual figure emerges from an environment that is pleasantly indistinct and, in the end, insignificant.

Speaking more generally, the visual aesthetics that dominate screens today tend to fall back upon perfectly delimited outlines. Under the regime of contour algorithms and 3D imaging, the figure no longer inhabits the image but is detached from it. The embedded shape no longer moves through spaces but in front of them, as if in front of a backdrop.

As the expression of alienation or increasing individualization, this trend also marks the rejection of what makes up the material richness of the cinematic image: its predisposition to avoid being fixed, defined, finished. If, as Jean Epstein proposes, cinema—the medium "of the variation of all relations in space and time, of the relativity of measurement, of the instability of all reference points, of the fluidity of the universe"—is a "form of thinking," it is not a Cartesian kind of thought but one shaped by the fluctuation and the incompleteness of things.[26]

In its most conventional guise, cinematic language has habituated us to consider the passage from blur to sharpness as a form of actualization. This is the classically Aristotelian trajectory: The blurred form and the image in motion are only the substrate of the sharp, stable image in which (ideally) they are fully achieved and become stabilized.

Blur in cinema exists indeed in relation to the sharp image, in a complex rapport that is shaped by a multiplicity of figures of appearance and disappearance, but this does not mean it is reducible to a dialectic between the visible and the invisible. Blur that exists not in service of a potentially sharper image but for itself confronts the spectator with "the test of non-knowledge."[27] From the *je ne sais quoi* of soft contours to the jumble of the unformed, between solid and liquid, the photographic and the pictorial, the appeal of blur stems from the principle of uncertainty. Since it excludes all the unrealized forms of the blurry image, is it not in fact the sharp image that is, ultimately, the impoverished one?

Definition

"The definition of blurriness": a paradox in terms. At the very least, however, we might attempt to specify what blur is not. Blur is what is not sharp or clear, what has no stable contours or precise outlines. From the fleeting to the foggy, blur thus takes the form of a multiplicity of appearances that are not necessarily degrees of figuration; abstract cinema, which works with effects of matter and light, is rich in gaseous atmospheres, fogged forms, precipitates of colors. Let us suppose, to take an example, that during a projection of *Rhythmus 21* (Hans Richter, 1921), the projector is badly adjusted and the edges of the geometric forms lose their sharpness. The effect would be completely different than the one intended by the filmmaker. In the movie theater, fans of experimental cinema would cry foul, as does Nanni Moretti in his *Diary of a Moviegoer* (2007).

The temporal factor renders the effects of cinematographic blur even more elusive. Filmed over time, a shot might include completely distorted images that evolve progressively toward a blurred figure and then a clear one, or vice versa. Depending on the case, such a shift could affect a part or the whole of the image, without the eye (even with the help of the pause button) being able to precisely identify the instant or the place of passage from one state to the other.[1] If image-sound synchronization in narrative cinema has singularly limited the possibilities of experimenting with blurriness, recorded sound is no less inclined to confusion, parasitic noise, static, and other rustles and hums. Take, for example, the obsessive and frustrated listening conducted by the protagonist of *The Conversation*, a surveillance expert supposed to have mastered advanced sound-recording technologies. *The Conversation* also offers a veritable compendium of visual blur, employing a telephoto lens, special effects (the artificial fog of the dream sequence), and natural filters (a dirty window, curtains, and various coverings). Visual and sonic blur here return constantly to a profoundly cinematic logic of perception and appearances: seeing, hearing, doubting. But Coppola's film is also the product of its historical setting. Imbued with the legacy of Hitchcock, born out of a particular political context, *The Conversation* is typical of 1970s American cinema, operating under a sort of paranoiac "interpretive delusion" fed by Abraham Zapruder's grainy images of the assassination of President Kennedy and exacerbated by the Watergate scandal.[2]

Variable and aleatory, the borders of blur are not always the domain purely of perception. Making them out is all the more contingent because they fluctuate depending on the era, technological support, and filmmaker.

Aesthetics of Blur

A return to an age of innocence: Seated between her mother and father, a very small child eats her meal in the garden of a house of which we see only a portion of a wall but which we can assume is a comfortable one. A light wind circulates from background to foreground, toying with branches, leaves, and the mother's hair and lifting the baby's lace collar.

Thanks to depth of field and to the reflections in the windows that occupy the left side of the frame, the film offers nice contrasts in definition, especially in its rendering of the vegetation that fills the Lumière family's garden. In the middle ground, the leaves of a fig tree that sways behind the baby's seat are recognizable by their fine outlines. In the background, on the other hand, the leafy mass that moves in the wind appears as a fluttering mass. Does this qualify as blur? If we can make the distinction, following Prosper Hillairet, between the trembling of the leaves in *Le repas de bébé* and the true "visual scrambling" orchestrated in the famous fairground scene in Jean Epstein's *The Faithful Heart* (1927), this distinction is not a simple difference in gradation but rather of distinct aesthetic orders.[1] For the Lumière brothers, blur is the sign of film's capacity to capture reality at its most fleeting—"a jumble of transient, forever dissolving patterns," as Siegfried Kracauer observes, emphasizing the Lumières' propensity for filming moving crowds and clouds of smoke.[2] For Epstein, on the other hand, blur is part of a stated artistic program. It is employed to de-realize the image; while it does account for the sensation of speed, it is also the representation of the onset of interior turmoil.

From the simple choice of subject to the most sophisticated stylistic effects, the practice of cinema as an art form gave rise to different aesthetics of blur very early on. In Soviet avant-garde film, as well as in films made as part of the Dada movement, blur represents the assertion of industrial modernity. The mark of the mechanical eye whose objective vision stretches beyond the range of ordinary human perception, blur imprints upon the filmic image movements that the human eye cannot capture; it suggests the existence of an optical unconscious that exceeds the individual. For French avant-garde and German expressionist filmmakers, in whose work modernity's appeal is tinged with existential doubt, blur is first and foremost the sign of a Romantic disposition. The blurred zone is where film abandons the simple observation of reality in order to explore subjective or interior states. The vision of the world presented in such films is filtered through dreams and emotions. Finally, in pictorialist or soft style, which developed in the United States in the lineage of photographic pictorialism, blur enhances the painterly qualities and atmospheric rendering of the cinematic image.

Of course, this brief historical panorama is reductive. The essence of blur is to resist dividing lines. The various stylistic schools and techniques intersect from the outset. Indeed, the attraction of blur in film arises from the contradictory richness of its effects. To film blur itself (fog, rain, speed) is to film what resists our gaze. To film blurrily (not to focus, to use a filter, to move the camera) is to veil, scramble, or disintegrate—so many ways of weakening human perception, but undertaken in order to orient it toward the sensory world. Between evanescence and opacity, blur sometimes pulls the image toward the immaterial (this is why ghosts tend to haunt the image's blurry zones) or toward matter (toward the pictorial, the place where the thickness and weight of things and bodies become tangible). Blur is the inscription of a body and its rhythms on screen (the shaky camera), as well as its negation (a car or a train speeding away). Blur is sensation; it is vision sliding toward touching, the perception of exterior chaos—but it is also the manifestation of the mental image, of dream or memory.

As the infinitely variable measure of a cinema that "in its visual expression has no limits," blur draws the filmic image into an open artistic field.[3] Blur that affects the whole of the image scrambles the border between cinema and painting; blur of apparition (focus blur) returns film to its origins in photochemical photography, to the progressive emergence of the image in the developing bath.

Rain, Mist, Fog

To our twenty-first-century eyes, accustomed to high-definition projections and the feel of the HD digital image's pronounced differentiations (absolutely sharp sharpnesses and completely blurry blurs, with perfectly controlled transitions between), images in films from the beginnings of the cinema can often, to varying degrees, seem dull and imprecise. Yet the absence of definition is comparable to the progressive erasure of memory; it shows the age of a film. In early cinema, indefinition also worked to trouble the border between the filmic universe and the viewer's, transforming the movie theater into an extension of the screen.

Silent cinema was partial to dawns and dusks, landscapes shrouded in fog or drenched with rain. The effect of such scenes is dramatic atmosphere: If they perhaps conceal the artificiality of cheap sets, they also, consciously or not, create the conditions for a mise en abyme in which the world on screen serves as the slightly distorted double of the world of the movie theater. The imaginary film projection staged by F. W. Murnau in *Sunrise* (1927) through a skillful system of transparencies is a striking example. Beneath a fake moon shining like a projector, a temptress arrived from the city tries to seduce a farm worker, extolling the attractions of the urban world. The eloquent description she gives him of the city's nightlife magically materializes in the form of projected moving images. On the screen that rises in the middle of the reeds appears an oneiric vision of urban life, foggy as the edges of the lake where the two lovers huddle to watch the spectacle. We perceive the distant echo of those early screenings in which images vibrated with the physical speed of the unrolling filmstrip and where clouds of cigarette smoke would rise to obscure the screen on which the film, sometimes already deteriorated or dusty, was projected.[1]

Siegfried Kracauer, who was particularly attuned to the interface between the film's world and the viewer's, referred not to a film's atmosphere but used instead liquid metaphors. The "world from above trembled in a dirty puddle": In his preface to *Theory of Film*, he describes his very first experience of film as a persistent memory of a reality reflected vaguely in the surface of water, a ghostly double printed on the film whose wavering image the projector conjured onscreen. "There was in the foreground," he writes, "a puddle reflecting invisible house façades and a piece of the sky. Then a breeze moved the shadows, and the façades with the sky beneath them began to waver." These images that "thrilled [Kracauer] deeply," and that "never left" him, seem to come straight out of a Joris Ivens film.[2]

To make *Rain* (1929), Ivens spent two years collecting images. From the first drops that ripple the surface of the canals to the water that trickles, then streams, down the tramway windows, to the glints of sun on the wet pavement, the film is a veritable compendium of recorded blurs. Ivens multiplies the angles of his shots, framing a bit of the canal agitated by the rain into concentric circles, the pointillist rendering of a tree in a puddle, a patch of shining asphalt in which hurrying passersby are reflected as deformed shapes. Seen from the rooftops, enveloped in mist, or shot from the steamy window of a tramway, Amsterdam takes on a spectral appearance.

The wet and quivering version of the urban symphony, *Rain* transforms the banal spectacle of an urban afternoon interrupted by a storm into an extraordinary composition where proliferating reflections produce a form of filmic mise en abyme. Its images also waver between the past and the present, the real city and the imagined one.[3] The historical city (brick houses with old gables) and its contemporary double (new methods of fast transport, the crowd of hurried city dwellers) are reflected and reformed in the puddles and on the surface of the canals disturbed by the falling drops. In the time it takes for a gust of wind to open the heart of urban space to the forces of nature, the film erects the vacillating portrait of a city where the past and modernity coexist: a multiplicity of jumbled impressions tinged with melancholy by the trembling reflection of the old world on the brink of disappearing.[4]

If cinematic blur is at the heart of modern vision, then the role it plays is ambiguous, caught between the exaltation of speed, shock, and sensation and the expression of the uncertainties that emerge in the wake of modernity. Certainly, the fumes that emanate from factories and the smoke that envelops big cities stand as the sign of an era in which humankind gains—at the price of anonymity—a certain freedom.

But in such misty or foggy conditions, framing and movements (of the camera as well of things and people) lose their meaning and function, and the narrative stalls. Stasis and the absence of perspective evoke the blocked horizons of those the mechanics of "progress" exploit and leave behind; melancholy and irrationality surface.

Fog, whether natural or artificial, creates a zone stripped of reference points or landmarks, where imagination must supplement vision. Genre cinema knows this fact well, using it as a device of suspense and anxiety, a bottomless expanse whose treacherous thickness hides murderers and the most fantastical monsters. In poetic realist dramas, fog casts a deceptive veil over the trap into which the hero on the run fatally stumbles.

In midcentury art cinema, characters become lost in fog so as to better confront the existential void. In Theo Angelopoulos's films, mist progressively becomes the privileged allegory for a lacunary collective history—that of the twentieth century, punctuated by catastrophes yet marred by amnesia. For Michelangelo Antonioni, it is the present and a certain idea of modernity that are in question. In his films, fog is the materialization of an existential lack. *Red Desert* (1964) contains a classic example with its strange tableau vivant, filmed in the murky swampland of the industrial zone outside Ravenna. Standing on a pier swallowed up in fog, the characters wait as if petrified. A thickening mist envelops their silhouettes; the figures start to disappear, becoming ghostly. The fog erases their shapes, and the racking of focus does the rest: Eyes become shadowy holes, heads become skulls, the tableau vivant becomes vanitas.

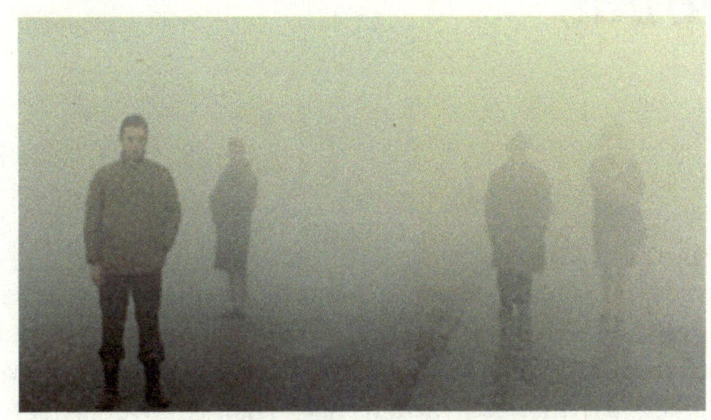

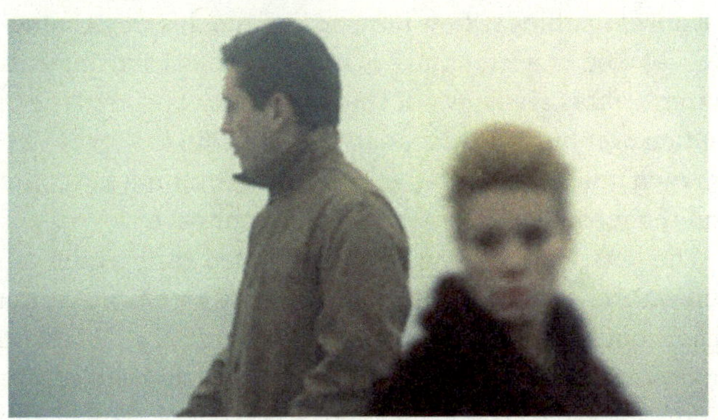

Focus

The relationship between fog and blur is pleonastic. When fog fills the screen, technology becomes redundant—it tends to disappear, to slide behind the natural phenomenon. Yet unlike the human eye, the lens needs neither myopia nor fog to see blurrily: "The camera lens . . . this false eye, can do so, but only according to how it is used."[1] Seen this way, cinematic blur—willed or accidental—is not a technical slip. Instead, it demonstrates an aspect of the superiority of cinematic perception over human perception—"a powerful eye that extends our own much too limited one"—in determining the content and the form of what appears before our gaze.[2]

The lens, that machine eye, fascinated early avant-garde filmmakers not because of its capacity to imitate human vision but because of its capacity to extend it. Where the human eye focuses automatically, the lens has a choice: There is no longer one vision, one unique perception, but an entire palette of possible renderings that would give a multitude of possible interpretations of the same object. Dziga Vertov demonstrates this in *Man with a Movie Camera* (1929), documenting the working of the lens in a brief sequence that forms the heart of the film. The lens itself appears in close-up, in a series of shot/reverse shots that leave out the cameraman and point to the camera as the origin of vision. A sort of *deus ex camera*, the lens controls and manipulates our perception of reality via the closing of the diaphragm and the alignment of its lenses.

The reverse shot at first appears as an assortment of white spots with hazy outlines: cotton balls, clouds, lumps of dough? Once the mechanism of the lens is adjusted, the demonstration's object is revealed by the magic of focus. In a progressive passage from blurriness to sharpness, the spots become branches of lilacs waving in the wind—or, more precisely, as the black background suggests, their negative image. The fact

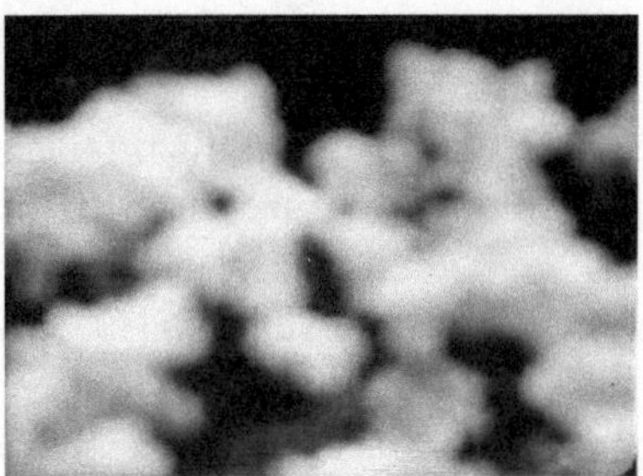

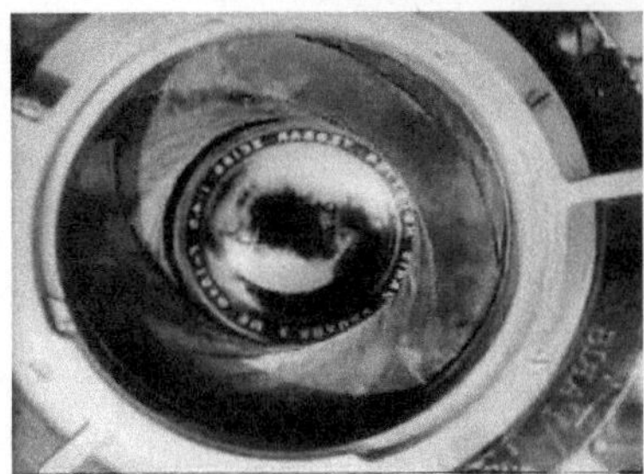

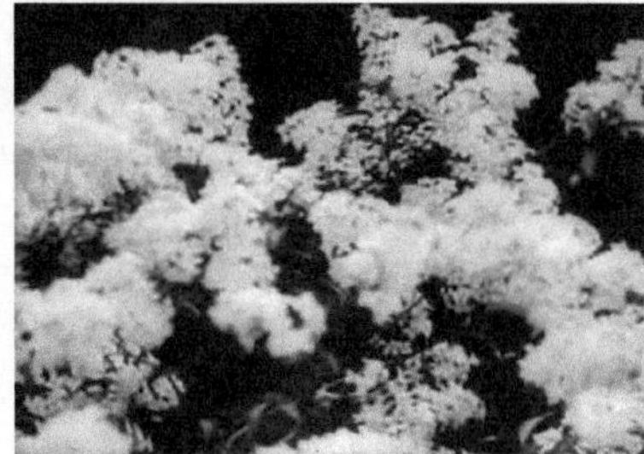

that these are modest branches does not diminish the effectiveness of the exercise. What counts is the process, the transformation of reality and the mechanics of desire (to see, to know) brought about and controlled by the lens.

Alfred Hitchcock:
Blur, or the Staging of Desire

The operations of focus amplify the miracle of on-screen presence, as well as the imminence of disappearance, modulating thresholds of visibility and invisibility, emphasizing and holding back the emergence of figures on the screen or their return to the unformed area of blur. In so doing, focal work plays on the viewer's desire.[3] In *Vertigo* (1958), Alfred Hitchcock, filmmaker of the scopic drive par excellence, literally lays bare the synergy between desire and the transition from blurriness to sharpness.

The use of blur in Hitchcock's films often takes conventional forms: an abundance of transparencies and dissolves, apparent myopia (*Strangers on a Train* [1951], *Spellbound* [1945]), vertigo and dizziness (*The Lady Vanishes* [1938], *Vertigo*, *North by Northwest* [1959]). But the difficulty that affects the viewer is far from simply a byproduct of the subjective point of view. Blur in Hitchcock's cinema plays a more insidious role. Its presence is sometimes felt without it being visible to the naked eye, as in the shower scene in *Psycho* (1960), where the addition of blurred frames imperceptibly intensifies the sensation of chaos and the impact of the deadly violence exerted on the victim's body.[4] On the other hand, blur is obvious in the no less famous episode in *Vertigo* of Judy's transformation into Madeleine. Here, the filmic image seems to take account of its own process of apparition.

Everything works together to make *Vertigo* into a great film of blur: its convoluted plot, its main character's fear of heights, of course, but also the place—San Francisco and its foggy bay—as well as certain formal choices: the captivating spirals of Saul Bass's credit sequence, the Technicolor and VistaVision cinematography that cancels out depth of field in tightly framed shots. Seen for the first time in Ernie's restaurant, for instance, chiseled against a blurred background, Kim Novak's profile takes on the cold delicacy of a cameo in its crimson velvet-lined box.

Exemplary of *Vertigo*'s nebulous, mystifying universe, the famous hotel sequence hinges on an impressive effect of partial blur that combines successive acts of refocus and reframing with a progressive fog-effect filter. The passage from blurriness to sharpness, which allegorizes the power of desire, incarnates both the hero's demiurgical fantasy and that of the director, since Judy/Madeleine is also, as Truffaut has noted, Kim Novak/Grace Kelly. The premise of the scene is well known: Judy is alone in the bathroom to complete her metamorphosis. When she reappears at the back of the room, now dressed and made up as Madeleine, she is, at first, nothing more than a vague figure encircled in green light—an unreal halo, with deathly connotations, that is nonetheless seemingly cast by the neon light that decorates the façade of the hotel where the scene takes place. Ghostly, a blur at the center of a sharp image, the silhouette of the young woman emerges and solidifies like a photographic print in a developing bath. In the series of shot/reverse shots that follow, the progressive reframing of Judy is accompanied by a reversal of the sharpness ratio: In a tight shot then in close-up, the young woman appears more and more in focus, and the background becomes blurrier.

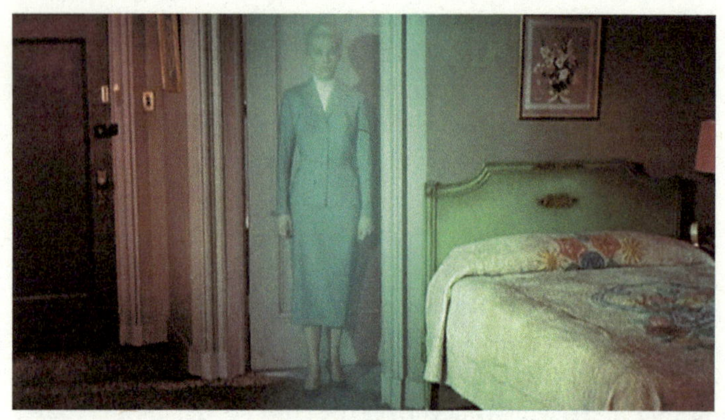

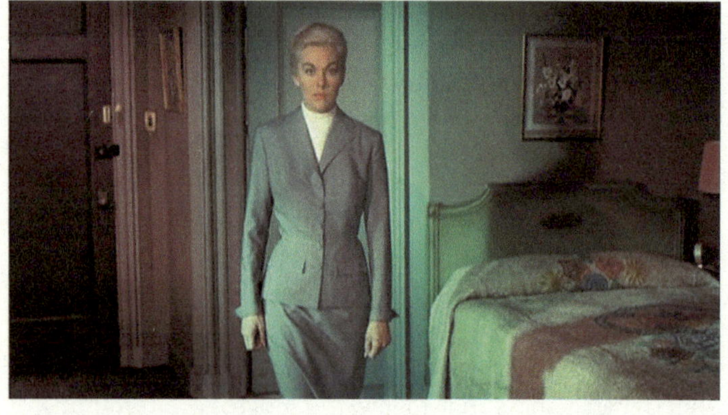

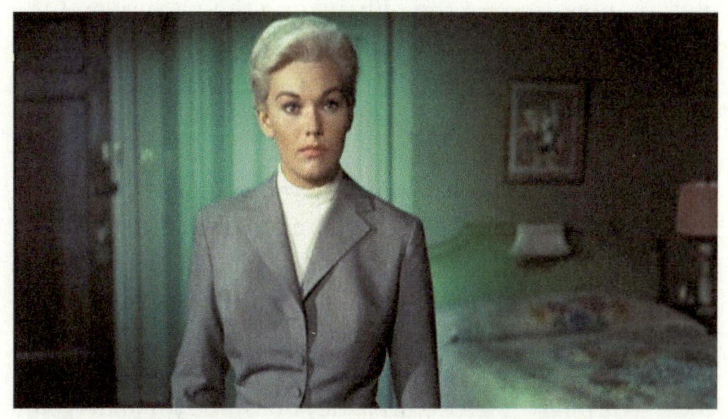

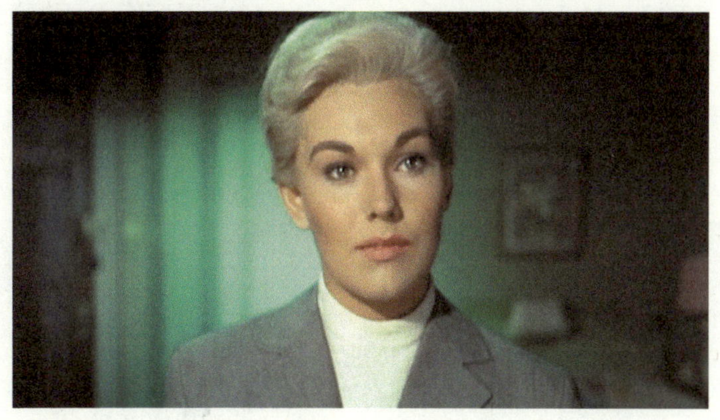

In this way, the subterfuge that determines Judy's recreation of Madeleine is echoed in how the shot decomposes, showing its own artifice. But beyond the wonder produced by the apparition, in the blurry zone the ghostly and the unformed are lurking. What is it, exactly, that emerges at first from the inanimate matter, this loosely outlined shape, caught in the wood of the door, in the green of the image?

Even in the context of classical narrative cinema, Hitchcock recognized the power of the camera's gaze to make and unmake the human. He not only employed these effects to seduce or terrify the viewer; he had fun with them.

Televised interlude: "This misty bit of ectoplasm, forming on the inside of your television screen, is one Alfred Hitchcock." The image is very blurry, the shot static yet undergoing transformation. Little by little, a human form emerges. Yet contrary to the progressive apparition of Madeleine, the shot does not return us to the image's photographic origin but to the effect of "morphing" instead.[5]

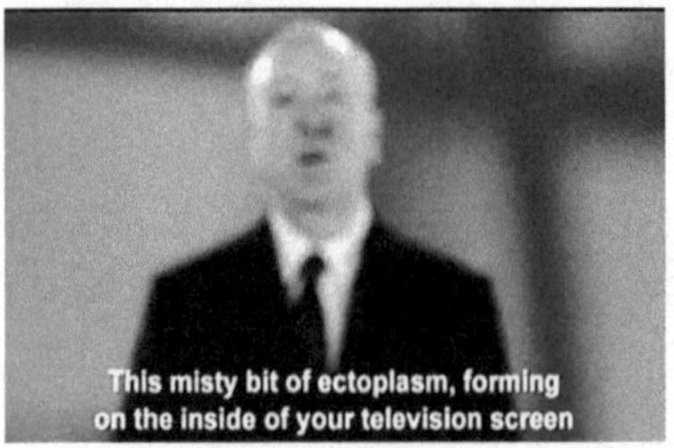

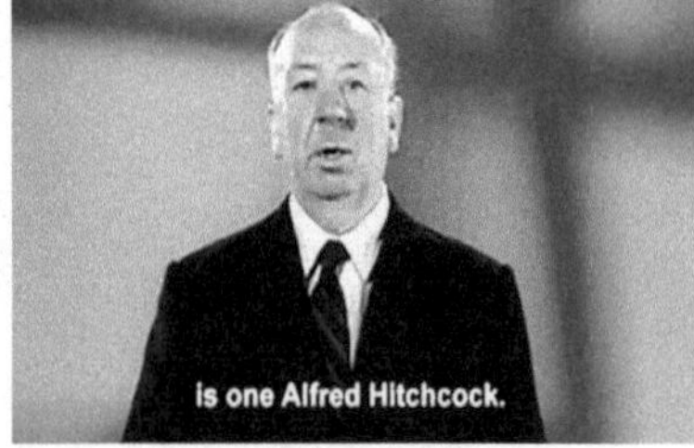

Alain Cavalier: Seeing Closer

Far from Hollywood's dream factory, Alain Cavalier also evokes the desire to see, but in his own way and from his point of view as a nearsighted filmmaker. This nearsightedness has no doubt helped shape his filmmaking practice: that of a cinema of closeness, characterized by an attention to detail and an interest in the spectacle of life in its most modest manifestations. One of the portraits he shot for his second series of documentaries about women and their careers (24 *Portraits d'Alain Cavalier*, 1991) is of an optician. The filmmaker uses the occasion to describe the fear of blindness that has plagued him since childhood and, by way of introduction, recounts witnessing his father losing his vision, his eyes filling with the fog of a glaucoma attack while he was driving.

Before he films her at work, Cavalier asks the optician to pose, framing her in a close-up. The camera focuses on her face, which occupies the center of the frame. The depth of field is shallow: On the right, the shop's display of a collection of frames is in focus, but in the background, the window and the street behind it are blurred. The filmmaker's voice, close and informal, explains: In the images that follow, he will try to show what it is like to be nearsighted. Operated manually, the lens zooms in on the model by degrees, without Cavalier using the focus that would let him (as in a conventional zoom) adjust the sharpness according to the modification of the framing and focal distance. The optician's face progressively fills the frame and is transformed, softening, giving first the look of an impressionist portrait, then losing its outline and its features altogether, suggesting a tachist work, before finally becoming an indistinct whole, a soup of diluted colors.

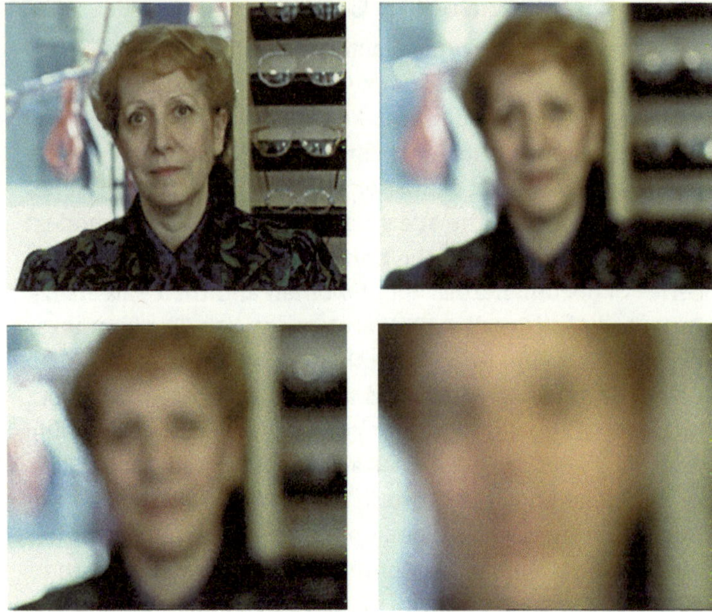

Cavalier describes the process of defiguration at work: "The features blur ... but you can still see her smile. It's nice ... it's in the gaze ... when you have lost the gaze of someone who you love, it's hard not to be able to see." What breaks down in blur is the proof of humanity and expressivity that usually, by a mirroring effect, triggers the onlooker's recognition, empathy, and identification with what they see. When there remains of the optician's face no more than a diluted surface, the image shifts not into abstraction but into formlessness: If the close-up is supposed to isolate and highlight the face, the incarnation of the subject, the overall blurriness ultimately turns it into undifferentiated matter instead.

The effacement of outlines here is accentuated by the distortions of scale and distance created by the zoom—a disregulated zoom, which flattens perspective and gives the impression of growing proximity while blurring details. But neither the illusion of proximity nor the tactile properties of the blurred image can appease the anguish of loss of vision. The filmmaker, at a given moment, catches himself turning the lens the wrong way: The process has reversed, and the image is becoming sharp again. "Ah! I moved backward—but now forward again," he exclaims. And the camera's eye zooms closer, "approaching" as if to touch—but to touch what? For the more the face fills the screen, the more its features and contours disappear, the more it tends toward the vaporous, transforming into something impalpable and vaguely abject.

Seeing [and] Touching

To see, Merleau-Ponty suggests, is to exercise a power of ubiquity, to be at once in the place from which one sees and to project oneself toward what is looked at. Vision, he says, is "palpation by looking."[6] But there is the presence of blur to be reckoned with, altering our perception of distances and consistencies. The eye perceives objects that are very far away or very close as blurry, as well as those whose substance fluctuates in the state of liquid or gas. To mobilize the effects of blur against the habits of ordinary perception means upsetting both the organization of space and the relationship between seeing and touching. Cavalier's demonstration begins with the gaze—the gaze of the lens that has the power to render all viewers myopic. In *Deconstructing Harry* (1997), Woody Allen also takes on this figure and offers his own comic version of the chaos of perception that blur creates.

Mel, an actor by trade, has become blurry. He discovers his state—an unusual situation that could cost him his job—on set. It is the cameraman who first realizes the metamorphosis has occurred. No matter how much he checks the state of his lens and changes the focal length, around the actor the set is perfectly clear, while Mel's silhouette resists efforts at focusing; its outlines and features remain indistinct, its appearance ectoplasmic. Mel's unfortunate state gives rise to perplexity, worry, and hilarity among his friends. His shape lacks definition; his contours look soft. For his children, who burst out laughing at him, he has stopped being a figure of authority.

The scene takes full advantage of the destabilizing powers of blur, which undoes the integrity of the human form, suggesting a subject in a state of dissolution. Not only is the affected area of the image here at the center of the frame, but it disturbs our ordinary perception of the body as a solid mass contained within its own skin. The vision of Mel's wife caressing his face, her hand sinking slightly into the blurred area, is deeply troubling. If to touch is to experience a border, to be in contact with the edges of a solid body, then blur deprives vision of the proof of actual touch.[7] In the gap between what we are given to see and what we believe, between the (soft) appearance of ectoplasm and the (firm) consistency that touch suggests, uncertainty sets in.

Through its use of technology, horror cinema has increasingly sought to exploit this ambiguity. To create the ghost in

Pulse (2001), Kiyoshi Kurosawa employs the same technique as Allen—rotoscoping—but in a digital version.[8] This ghost has a human form, but in the pale oval of its face only the eyes are clear, shining with demonic intensity. The fright the image occasions stems from the impossibility of qualifying it or evaluating its degree of materiality or immateriality, especially since in *Pulse*, as in *Deconstructing Harry*, the background remains sharp around the smear of the ghostly figure. Kawashima, *Pulse*'s protagonist, doesn't believe in ghosts, and so he makes the gesture that any viewer, like a powerless Saint Thomas, wishes for as much as they fear: To demonstrate the

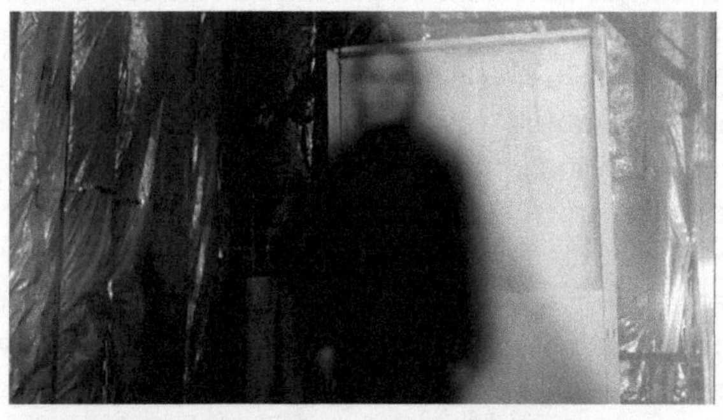

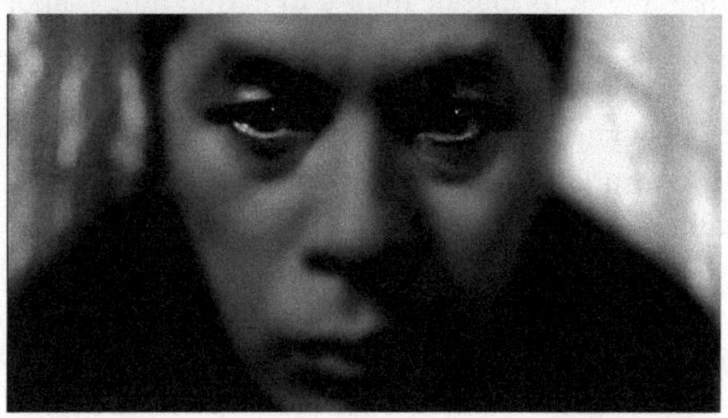

ghost's nonexistence, he touches it. As in *Deconstructing Harry*, it is the mismatch between seeing and touching that produces the scene's strangeness. The ghost is blurry; our eyes, as well as our knowledge of the classic ghost—the ghost that appears via superimposition and has the good taste to stick to the immateriality that its diaphanous look suggests—tell us that there is no real physical presence. But what Kawashima's hand encounters, instead of slipping through, does have a consistency. Contaminated by his contact with the specter, the young man is swallowed into limbo.

In both *Deconstructing Harry* and in *Pulse*, blur spreads like a virus. Allen's film contains nested narratives: The episode that Mel enacts is a scenario imagined by Harry, a vividly imaginative writer. Yet the "illness" of blur overflows from one fictional universe to another. Soon it affects Mel's creator, who, struck by anxiety, realizes that his own appearance, like that of his character's, is lacking definition.

Even more than in *Pulse*, where the generic expectations prepare the viewer to doubt their own eyes, the images in *Deconstructing Harry* are disconcerting because they reverse the conventional order of appearances. Blur here does not carry out any of its classical uses in fiction film, responding to the requirements of realism or staging. No longer relegated to the near foreground or the far background but existing as a sort of open wound at the heart of the image, upsetting its entire composition, blur becomes a powerful tool of defamiliarization.[9]

The Tactile Eye

Canceled perspective, forms and colors that alternately dissolve and diffuse or reform, which condense and detach from the background: When, in the fluctuations between blurriness and sharpness, the process of appearance and disappearance is deployed in the course of a shot, the sensory experience of the image is intensified, and vision opens onto other senses.

When seeing even the most normative film on the big screen, it is rare that the pleasure produced by the variations in degrees of definition, grain, distance, and depth of field is entirely absent. But it is when, against or in spite of habituation, the passage from blur to sharpness is rendered, even momentarily, perceptible that we become aware of how the fluctuations in focus affect our senses.

The pleasure we experience when the cinematic image alternates between the sharpness of distanced vision and the blurred image that evokes proximity (the point at which the eye no longer has sufficient distance to focus) is comparable to the pleasure produced by certain collages in which fragments from a variety of materials, chosen for their textures, stand alongside figurative elements that have been rendered precisely and according to the rules of perspective. In film, certain forms of montage using collage effects also play on the contrast between interpretive vision (a "reading" of the image) and tactile vision (the eye as it "grazes" the surface of the image, to use Paul Klee's word).

From modern Hollywood cinema, one might think of Norman Jewison's clever usage of the split screen for the sequences of the polo match and the bank holdup in *The Thomas Crown Affair* (1968). For the former, a kaleidoscopic and gripping representation of polo players in action dynamically combines optical and kinetic blur with fragments of sharper images. The images appear within internal frames of variable size that slide from one side of the screen to another or that multiply to the point of scattering into vertiginous duplicates of the same shot (like contact sheets or serigraphy, but animated). Here the blur of dispersion fuses with focus blur.

The second sequence of split screens is presented as a puzzle version of parallel montage: Blurred or clear images of a gang of robbers whose various trajectories converge at the bank permutate, with no apparent logic, on a screen resembling an irregular checkerboard. The effect is less to destabilize the visual field than to distill information and create suspense, yet the effectiveness and the power of seduction of this aesthetic, which lies somewhere between pop art and advertising, is undeniable. Between the shimmering blurred insets and the profusion of details in the sharper shots, the surface effects and the depth of field that draws in the gaze, a panoply of sensations are offered to an eye that wanders across the segmented screen. By juxtaposing images of the same sequence at radically different degrees of resolution, *The Thomas Crown Affair* enacts a veritable staging of the image's modes of apparition: The intrigue is as much visual as narrative.

One detail, however, anchors us firmly in the system of classical film narration: Each of these split-screen sequences includes shots of a character holding a pair of binoculars or a camera, as if to refute—by attributing it to a precise point of view—the suprahuman aspect of this reconstitution of the real by an augmented, multiple, and omniscient vision that encompasses both blurriness and clarity.

Motion Blur

Like focus blur, motion blur—blur produced by speed, by the movement of a mobile point of view, or by the movement of filmed bodies or objects—makes tangible the thresholds of visibility that mark the limits of human perception.

From the outset, the Lumière brothers understood that in order to capture and reproduce movement fluidly (differently, then, from chronophotography or futurist photography), the ideal of perfect sharpness would have to be sacrificed. Genre film continues to operate on this intuition, while new generations of video games also now integrate motion blur to prevent the "jerky recomposition of movement" as already advised in the users' manual for the Lumière cinématographe.[1]

But if the viewer senses blur's absence in the jerkiness of movement recomposed uniquely from sharp shots, they nevertheless do not consciously register the blur of what moves. The camera, on the other hand, can record it, and film can reproduce it; the spectator is then carried along, in a mixture of exaltation and dispossession, by the spectacle of a world that speeds by.

Speeds

As the expression of the new fusion between vision and sensation enabled by the filmic machine, motion blur is at the heart of modern perception. Whirling, spinning, crumbling, pistons and wheels turning at top speed, landscapes that fall away under the effect of acceleration, the "unchained camera" that twirls or flies off: Avant-garde filmmakers worked to give the viewer an experience of reality that had previously been impossible to represent.[2] Nourished by the fascination with movement and speed, such a goal engendered a proliferation of experiments and a vast palette of blurs, from the scrambled to the fleeting.

Yet if speed and motion blur—and especially the moving point of view, representing the speed of the machines carrying the immobile bodies of travelers—work together to extend the limits of human perception, they also signal the obsolescence of the latter. It is through blur that the paradox unique to this new type of vision is made manifest: Certainly, movement carries with it the promise of seeing more, and more intensely, yet the increasing speed of appearance of the visible world makes it impossible to perceive things fully. Like the train passenger who can only see precisely what stretches out in the distance, the avid spectator of new horizons must be resigned to the fact that a part of the visual field escapes them.[3]

To introduce the camera "into the heart of the spectacle of life," letting it dangle suspended by a cable, throwing it in the air, or attaching it to the saddle of a horse spurred to a gallop: Abel Gance's inventiveness with the camera's mobility and the orchestration of movement remains unparalleled. Yet although they accord with the modernist ambitions of the filmic avant-gardes, Gance's films nevertheless remain dedicated to recreating the subjective experiences of their characters. They also take account of the confrontation between two visual regimes, a confrontation in which the triumph of movement, speed, and sensation occurs at the expense of a space-time of which the human had formerly been the measure. The train conductor Sisif, the protagonist of *La roue* (1923), is the embodiment of this conflict: Burned by a steam jet, he becomes almost blind.

One of *La roue*'s most remarkable sequences is the one in which Sisif conducts the train that is taking his adoptive daughter to Paris, where she is to be married. To translate the character's despair, which pushes his locomotive to extreme speed, as well as the fright of the young passenger who is captive in the racing train, Gance multiplies shots of the train's exterior and interior in an accelerating montage. Wheels and pistons spin at top speed, clouds of smoke rise from the smokestack, the rails stream by, the wheels again, the pistons, the rails: The shots follow one another faster and faster until they are indistinguishable. By the sequence's end, montage intensifies motion blur to the point where the film itself seems to shake.

The contrast with the scene of arrival in Paris is striking: A long shot replaces the quick montage, and the vibration of motion blur gives way to the ominous feel of atmospheric blur. In the declining light of the end of the day emerges the bulky shape of the station into which the locomotive is heading, enveloped in smoke.

Unlike Gance's fictions, Ivens's films keep to a strictly documentary point of view. His celebration of modernity, however, is also nuanced by a touch of melancholy that signals a consciousness of the ravages of time. In *The Bridge* (1927–1928), as in *Rain*, two regimes of blur coexist: At the edges of the tumultuous zone of blurriness caused by speed and in the softness of the foggy backgrounds persists the sfumato trace of a world destined to disappear.

The principal role is not held, or not solely held, by the imposing steel edifice that gives the film its title but also by the train, that dynamic force with which the camera's gaze identifies. Ivens films the machine in all its aspects: In close-up shots, he pictures the wheels that turn and whose outlines blend into one another, as if soldered by speed; in vertiginous low-angle shots, he shows the steam jets that envelop the bridge's metallic structures in a vaporous haze. He also films from the moving train: Landscapes speed by, swallowed up by the swiftness of motion, scrambled to the point of abstraction. We cross the bridge at full speed, and the passage of the metal girders punctuates the foreground, giving the effect of optical flutter or flicker. The hardness of steel and the geometric sharpness of the structures both give way under the effect of this speed: The bridge's architecture is rendered here as a futurist succession of multiplying lines. In the background, however, extends—vaporous, pictorial—the outline of the port of Rotterdam, an untidy multitude of boats and barges. Made indistinct by distance, one can just make out horse-drawn carts alongside the trucks and cars moving in the bridge's shadow.

Thirty years later, the frontiers of modernity had shifted, leaving behind its old symbols, including the train. A new avant-garde was being born on the other side of the Atlantic.

In 1955, Joseph Cornell commissioned Stan Brakhage to make a film intended to document New York's Third Avenue elevated train before its demolition. The theme was itself not exceptional: As a source of inspiration, reservoir of forms, and field for experimentation, the urban cityscape of New York was the first subject of the growing American underground.[4] A generation of emerging filmmakers, armed with Bolex cameras, would capture it in a profusion of on-the-spot images, reviving something of the spirit of the city symphonies of the 1920s.

One of Brakhage's early works, *The Wonder Ring* is already a complex study of film blur, a stunning play of mirrored reflections in which Brakhage experiments with some of the effects he would later explore in more depth (motion blur and superimposition). The film alternates shots taken in stations and from platforms with shots filmed from inside the cars. Seen through the window of a moving train, the cityscape is doubly altered, disintegrating under the effects of speed and transformed by the irregularities of the window panes.

The street streams by, façade after façade, like a fan unfolding. Over the irregular unfurling of the buildings is overlaid the silhouette of a passenger, backlit and further obscured by the trembling, fluttering reflection that the light shining through the window projects onto the opposite window. The aesthetic richness of the film stems from the strata of images that are reflected from one window to the other and from the jumble of shimmering forms in which the origin of the gaze is lost: The filmmaker escapes in the crisscrossing of reflections. Despite the captivating complexity of its composition, *The Wonder Ring* is not just a formal exercise. It also evokes a uniquely urban nostalgia—an awareness of a present that is itself fleeing, at once modern and already out of date.

From the rail traveler to the space traveler: The logic of the dispossession of the visible, which conditions access to a suprahuman space-time, finds its ultimate expression in science fiction film. A filmmaker of melancholy and asynchronous destinies, Wong Kar-wai makes use of such logic almost to the point of mannerism in 2046 (2004), in which the windows of a train speeding toward nowhere show nothing of the exterior world besides a streaked surface. But it is the classic "Star Gate" sequence of 2001: A *Space Odyssey* (Stanley Kubrick, 1968) that first comes to mind, where an astronaut enclosed in a minuscule capsule is swallowed at incredible speed into a cosmic tunnel. The "slit-scan" technique, developed specially by Douglas Trumbull, transforms space into a ray of colored lines, the trajectory of which draws the gaze toward the center of the screen. The image tilts toward abstraction, ultimately escaping all reference to human perception.[5]

The ultra-accelerated, or time lapse, shot also suggests a suprahuman temporality that can be captured only by the machine, although less aggressively than the slit-scan. Paradoxically, the effect of acceleration is obtained by filming at a slower speed. Prolonged exposure time allows the traces of movement to be recorded: The contours of moving objects soften, colors meld together, and movements become trajectories. Fleeting traces connect the mobile form to its point of departure even as it reaches its destination, inscribing the passage of time into the image itself. From diurnal atmospheric variations to the streets of modern megacities lit by nighttime traffic, time lapse offers a vision of the urban environment from which the human figure is removed. Monuments and buildings, emblems of History and the persistence of certain forms of power, are durably inscribed into the image, while the living world is captured and represented in its unstable, transitory nature—the trembling shapes of trees, the shuddering of cars, the stream of light from headlights and taillights that traverses the city's arteries like a long blurry snake.

Slow Motion [Jean-Luc Godard]

What the blur of speed hides from human perception slow motion attempts to recapture, circumventing technology itself. In its classic form, slow motion results from a faster capture of images that are then projected at standard speed: Movement unfurls in a temporality that has become elastic.

Ostensibly, slow motion enables access to what is normally difficult to see with the naked eye: It allows for an analysis of each instant and for a study of the details of movement that would be invisible at normal speed. The interest it held for the inventors of chronophotography, as well as the reason for its widespread use in sports broadcasting today, stems from this ability. Yet the idea that we might simply slow down the shot and dissect it, reveling in its mysteries, ignores blur, which exists as an inherent component of filmed movement and is often revealed by slow motion.

Photography at high speed does, of course, sometimes have the power to eliminate blur. In some of Bill Viola's works, the use of extreme slow motion (300 images per second) produces a sort of petrification of the image.[6] In the absence of blur and of any instability of contours, the image is emptied of all movement. It also loses all power to move us: Even when the actors' bodies, as in *Silent Mountain* (2001), bend under the effects of intense pain, the appearance of their expressions and gestures resembles a physiognomic study.

The exaltation unique to cinematic slow motion, which commercial cinema has systematically used to the point of transforming into a cliché what for Vertov, Epstein, or Vigo was striking for its affective force, is inextricable from blur. The nineteen "orchestrated skids of the image"[7] in Jean-Luc Godard's *Every Man for Himself* (1980) are exemplary in this regard.

Blur occupies a singular place in Godard's filmography. Jump cuts in *Breathless* (1960); slow motion in *Every Man for Himself* (1980); solarization, optical effects, the saturation and diffusion of colors in *In Praise of Love*; visual and sonic superimposition in *Histoire(s) du cinéma* (1998); and deconstructed 3D in *Goodbye to Language* (2014): Shuddering, trembling, fleeting, superimposed or doubled, the blurry image appears in these crucial moments when the filmmaker experiments with new techniques, interrogating the potentialities of cinema in relation to other forms of media.

Every Man for Himself marks Godard's return to cinema after a long detour through television, where his slow-motion practice began. This return to film occurred in the context of a cinema in crisis, threatened by the increasing presence of the small screen and of video. Godard's response was both simple and radical: to denounce purely commercial uses of the image and the made-for-TV film, returning cinema to its expanded artistic field, in conversation with painting and photography.

Camera-as-paintbrush: Godard's long panoramas of Lake Geneva's foggy shores recall the German Romantics; the twilight skies tilt the image toward Turner's paintings. When suddenly the rhythm changes, the combination of slow motion with panning or tracking shots transforms the landscape into colorful interlacings and lines. In images that resemble the use of scraping techniques in painting (Gerhard Richter, for example), trees, roadsides, and skies full of clouds disintegrate into green, black, and blue streaks.

If some sequences seem to revive the old Dada dream of paintings in motion, *Every Man for Himself* nevertheless abandons neither figuration nor a commitment to cinema's photographic origins. The film's slowed passages lack the fluidity of classical slow motion. Unlike the fluid appearance of motion blur caught in long exposure, in *Every Man for Himself*'s slow motion sequences, the repetition or exclusion of images produces a strong impression of discontinuity. Shots unfurl through bumps and tremors (as when a film projector is sticking). With each jerk the basic component of film appears, the photogram—and with it, blur.

In its discontinuous slow-motion sequences, the film seems to return us at once to the serial dimension of futurist photographs, streaked with blur, and to fixed-plate chronophotography, which used long exposures to capture bodies in motion. Godard also cites Marey on the superfluity of filming at normal speed, since this is what we see all the time with our own eyes. Again, when it is used to dissect the movements of the human body, we might expect slow motion to undo their mysteries, revealing the microvariations of our

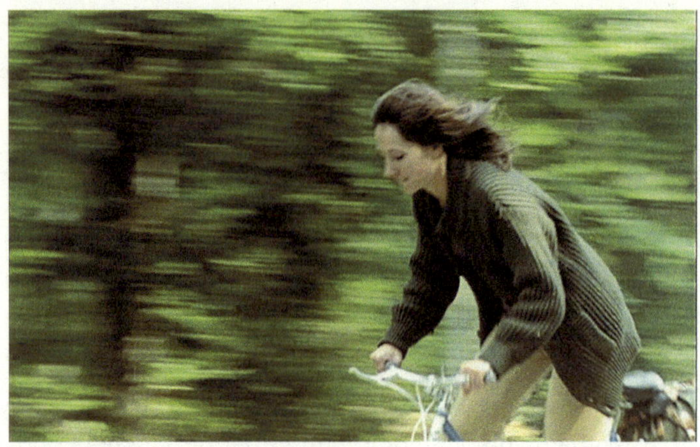

gestures. Yet this is in no way the case. Even in the most ordinary gestures, the most determined by the machine—those of the cyclist or the worker whom Godard films—there is an element of unpredictability, a sort of wavering produced by blur that accompanies movement and is magnified by slow motion. Between two moments of "concreteness,"[8] where movement is stabilized and the image becomes clear, blur thus preserves slight spaces of becoming, like so many points of resistance—an affirmation of the freedom to not be (defined, named, circumscribed).[9]

When Godard films a couple embracing, somewhere between attraction and aggression, he films it like a collision. The two people face each other across a kitchen table. Suddenly the man rises, throwing himself on the woman and putting his arms around her, then bringing her down with him. It is a way of evoking the impossibility of intimate and immediate relationships in a world ruled by commerce. But in its physicality, the scene exceeds metaphor: The embrace also expresses a shared desire for contact, clumsy and desperate. Shot in slow motion, the sequence is punctuated by microinterruptions, brief and slightly blurry freeze-frames that reveal film's photographic foundations. The panoramic movement of the camera accompanies the arc made by the bodies; the shot unfolds jerkily. The effect resembles the famous chronophotographs of boxers from the end of the nineteenth century—images intended for the scientific study of movement, of course, but that also testified to the desire to enter into the heart of bodily contact, to examine what happens at the moment of touch (the erotic charge of this kind of image did not escape Francis Bacon, painter par excellence of motion blur). But blur, too, exists at the heart of the image, at the point of contact between bodies, and keeps its secret.

We might see *Every Man for Himself* as a film of hopelessness, a definitive demonstration of the omnipresence of the capitalist machine: life, death, work, sex, like a filmic montage or montage sequence, a set of gears on which the characters have no purchase.[10]

Yet signs of resilience are also present, in the "trembling of features," in the "surges of irregularity" that exist in blur, which envelops the characters' gestures in a halo of indeterminacy.[11]

Movement, photography, painting: In *Every Man for Himself*, as in Godard's following films, blur is both the manifestation of the mobility and the becoming of forms *and* the erasure of the superfluous, the means by which the photographic meets the painterly.

Shakiness [Sally Potter]

In motion blur as in speed blur, the gain in sensation occurs at the price of losing part of the visual field. But whereas speed blur translates the point of view and mobility of the machine, motion blur resulting from a shaky camera promises to reinscribe the subject and the body into the heart of the film, since a trace of movement is transmitted by the operator to the camera.

Relatively rare in silent and classic films (Gance, tossing the camera into the middle of a snowball fight, serves as the exception),[12] shaky camera now stands as a new realist style, especially with the advent of light and hypermobile video cameras, followed by small and ready-to-film digital devices (and, in particular, mobile phones).[13] An increase in manipulability and mobility has led to a proliferation of unsteady filmmaking techniques that embody the forms of narcissism typical of contemporary regimes of vision. The image's instability not only aims at encouraging an intensified physical identification with the film's characters; the characters, the camera operator, and the camera itself are often united into one being, to the point that in horror films that employ this kind of blur, the death of one leads to the (mechanical) death of the other.

As early as the 1920s, Béla Balázs described this morbid relationship between the man and the camera, writing in *Theory of Film* of the war films that depict the death of the cameraman: "The camera wobbles, the image blurs, like dying eyes glazing over."[14] From *The Blair Witch Project* (1999) to *Cloverfield* (2008), contemporary fiction films have transformed this extreme manifestation of the identification between man and the apparatus into a cliché. But the prospect of death is exactly what such films pursue, camera in hand, and what the shaky camera lens keeps in its line of sight: Sequences of camera-carrying pursuit are now part of the requisite sequences of commercial action films. A shot is fired, the camera jumps as if from the recoil, and the border between film and video game is blurred.

Lucien Castain-Taylor and Véréna Paravel employ a similar logic of sensation for their film *Leviathan* (2012), but to different ends. Making innovative use of Go-Pro cameras, instead of documenting sports or war, the filmmakers capture the realities of industrial fishing aboard a commercial trawler. First fixed to the bodies of the fishermen, the cameras are then attached to the mast, the hull, or thrown in the sea and towed by the boat. The film is blurry, almost from end to end. Representing an indifferent, unanchored point of view, the antishock cameras spin, plunging into debris, mingling with the mess of fish carcasses, indiscriminately registering the devastating chaos caused by the blindly destructive presence of the human.

Yet when they first appeared, light and manipulable filming technologies possessed a utopic dimension that seemed to renew the modernist impulse of early cinema. Released from the need for bulky film storage, small electronic video cameras, followed by digital ones, promised both to popularize the practice of film and to open it to a less normative aesthetic. With the advent of the handheld camera, shaky filmmaking no longer stood as a mistake but instead signaled freedom, closeness, and increased sensorial immersion. It was in this spirit that, three years before two Danish filmmakers would humorously formalize these new aesthetic principles in their

"Dogme 95" manifesto, Sally Potter celebrated the emergence of a new type of filmmaking at the end of *Orlando* (1992).

Initially, *Orlando* seems to oppose painting (official portraiture, the pose, the reified body, the distanced point of view) and cinema (shooting with a handheld camera, the immersive point of view). The pictorial surfaces, however, in the confusion between the figural and the gestural in Potter's shaky motion blur. Not only does the film stage an alliance between the tactile aspect of things and the gesture of the artist-filmmaker, according to the "logic of sensation," but it also operates in the manner of action painting.

Orlando at first adheres to the visual codes of the standard historical adaptation film: sumptuous lighting, costumes, and settings; deliberately spectacular staging; and meticulous photography. Its conclusion, however, returns to the experimentation of the director's first films, giving Virginia Woolf's novel a contemporary epilogue. Orlando has lived for four centuries and become a woman. She has experienced the laws and prejudices that come with her new gender, as well as the constraints of the corset and the pannier dress, before finally freeing herself from a destiny that would have imposed social convention upon her.

In Potter's ending, we have reached the end of the twentieth century. Accompanied by her child, the hero-turned-heroine visits her former castle, which has been transformed into a museum. There she admires her own official portrait as a young man of the Elizabethan era. The embodiment of an obsolete system that thought itself to be immutable, this Orlando poses in a rigid doublet, adorned with all the ornaments befitting his rank.

The screen then fills with a magma of gray particles. The sound crackles, the kind of electrostatic interference characteristic of a video clip. What follows is a gorgeous tumult of blurred images, captured by a handheld video camera wading through tall grass. The sequence continues in the form of alternating shots on film (the objective point of view) and shots on video (the subjective). The author of the video images is inferred to be Orlando's child. Filmed in 35mm, she (or he?) runs through the field, little camera in hand. A succession of blurred images crosses the screen rapidly. Grasses, trees, sky: The movements of the body are transferred to the image via blurred arabesques. Colors mix and forms dissolve, tipping from solid toward liquid.

The marriage of media, the play with definitions and textures, the passage from stability to movement and from sharpness to blur: The film becomes collage, a celebration of the moving image in both its affinity with modern painting and in the new heterogeneity and dynamism that video brings. If Potter shoots the final frames in 35mm (a striking shot of Tilda Swinton looking directly at the camera), she nevertheless confers on the imprecise lens of the video camera the task of revealing the incongruous presence of the angel floating above the scene: Jimmy Somerville, suspended in midair, lends the supernatural being his androgynous voice and silhouette in a sequence joyously haunted by electrostatic.

A hymn to the hybrid, the transgender, and the transmedia, *Orlando*'s epilogue uses blur as a sign of freedom and renewal: the freedom of the film's main character, of course, but also—between film and video, between staging and filming spontaneous action—the possible revival of cinema.

Interlacings [Leighton Pierce]

In the same hybrid zone anticipated by Potter's film, the work of Leighton Pierce takes place at the intersection of experimental film and video.

In the words of the director and critic Jon Jost, Pierce can be seen as a "master miniaturist."[15] This designation can be understood in two ways. First, it emphasizes the filmmaker and video artist's propensity for using his short, non-narrative films to explore the universe that immediately surrounds him (Pierce often films his friends and families in domestic, circumscribed settings). But "master miniaturist" can also be understood in reference to the kind of minor cinema that Pierce pursues on the margins of commercial and experimental aesthetics. Between the exploration of intimacy and the development of a minor cinema, blur is a distinctive trait of Pierce's work, the foundation of a "synesthetic" deployment of the image where seeing and touching meet.

If his early photochemical films and his later digital videos have blur in common, this blur stems from the specific properties of each of the two mediums. Hence in his recent work, the blur of movement appears as a natural extension of the interlaced signals characteristic of the video image.

Pierce films with a handheld camera, with long exposure. Blur arises both from the movement of the camera and from the mobile objects whose trajectories are captured across time. It also results from a particular montage technique: His works are made up of layers, strata of images superimposed with slight discrepancies and then smoothed over, keeping the effects of layering while minimizing unevenness. The soundtrack, similarly, uses superposition, playing with a double register of extreme closeness (noises associated

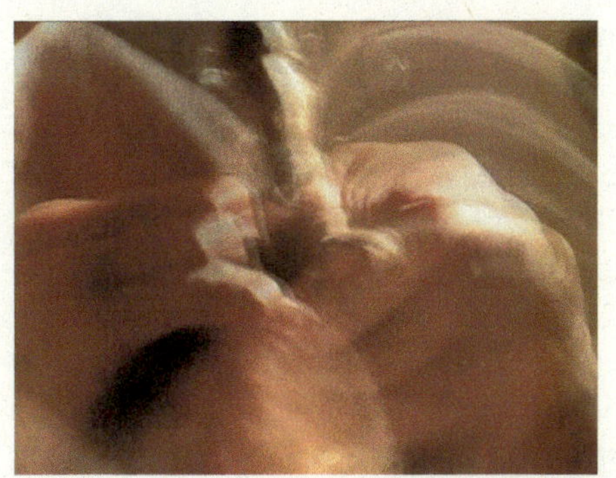

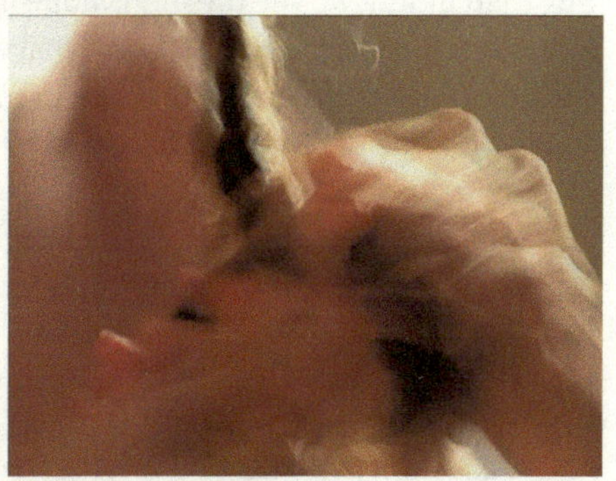

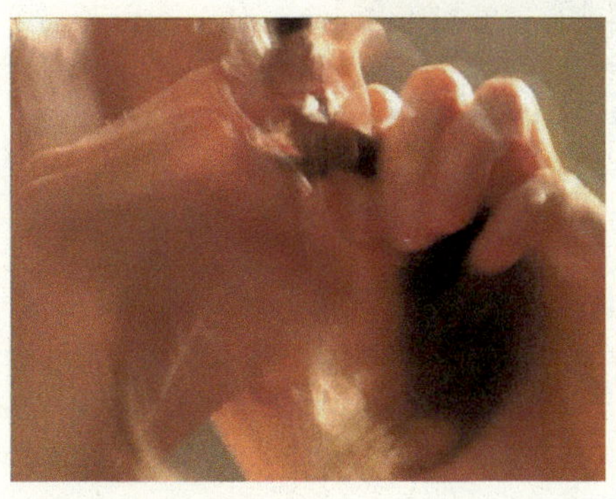

with the image's content) and far-off, vague murmurs and rumbles.

A sense of underlying connection infuses A *Private Happiness* (2003), a video portrait of a couple that forms a sort of antithesis to Godard's vision of the couple, which is driven by inevitable disjunction.

Pierce and his wife lend their own silhouettes to this couple, whose intimacy the film explores through a succession of domestic situations and gestures. The woman brushes her hair, showers, walks; then the couple is seen at night embracing; then finally we see the man, alone in his bed. The chronology is unclear, as is the nature of the images, which could be a kind of filmic journal or dreamlike memory.

Pierce films objects and bodies as closely as possible. The camera caresses their surfaces, lingering on details and gestures. The woman does her hair, running her fingers through it again and again, untangling then gathering and braiding it. Magnified by blur, the gesture echoes the filmmaker's technique: Pierce braids his images together, uniting them into a smooth and undulating flux in which distinctions between them dissolve.

The gaze is caught in this fluid and enveloping movement, punctuated by moments of fragile equilibrium. We pause for a brief moment, for instance, as the wandering lens stops on the graceful, if not completely solidified, position of the woman's bare feet.

What is more difficult to suggest via the visual image than closeness or physical intimacy, an embrace or an intertwining—the moments when the gaze loses its primacy in favor of the tactile sense?[16] Despite their differences (heavily retouched film for Schneeman, the dematerialized video image for Pierce), the images of Carolee Schneeman's *Fuses* (1967) haunt *A Private Happiness*'s night scenes: The camera meanders close to the bodies, but the blurred image reveals little, wavering at the limit of figuration and abstraction.

In Pierce's work, blur both intensifies the feeling of proximity, the takeover of seeing by touching, and veils the image's content, disarming the inquisitive eye. The possibility of a shared proximity thus depends on the renunciation of possession by the gaze. Irreconcilable in their formal and critical ambitions, Godard's film portrait of a couple and Pierce's video portrait do have one trait in common: Blur appears in them as the impossibility of perfect knowledge—and through knowledge, possession—of the other.[17]

Reveries of the Image

In motion blur and in the shaky camera, the cinematic image documents a complex relationship to the exterior world. To make perceptible the passage from sharpness to blurriness and back again, to point to thresholds of visibility, means drawing the viewer's attention to the mediation of the camera, as well as to the habits and limitations of the human eye. Hence paradoxically, technologically assisted vision and the progress of optical technologies have in fact reinforced the dimension of magic and mystery at the heart of the visual.

Indeed, if cinematic techniques such as blur give form to an external reality that is invisible or illegible to the naked eye, do they not also help us imagine the expression of an interior or unconscious vision, a kind of dreaming in images? Whereas precise outlines are the basis of ordinary perception and the mark of the alert, rational consciousness, does not blur instead evoke a dulling of the senses, a state of emotional absorption, a suppressed consciousness?

The use of blur to suggest what escapes the senses is, of course, not the prerogative or invention of cinema. It is already present in other media contemporaneous with film's beginnings. Late Victorian painting, the fantastical photography of the nineteenth century, and spirit photography all use effects of fading and superposition to evoke the psyche, dreams, and the world of ghosts. The temporal dimension of the moving image, however, lends specific suggestive force to the representation of the *passage* from consciousness to dream state. From the beginnings of cinema, transitional blur thus served to mark the instant at which dream and reality meet. George Albert Smith's *Let Me Dream Again* (1900) serves as a classic example: A man of a certain age has a drink with a beautiful young woman wearing a clown costume and eventually embraces her. Waking up, he finds himself in the bed he shares with his nagging wife, who scolds him for having unknowingly put his arm around her while sleeping. To make the story instantly comprehensible, a progressive lowering of focus plunges the end of the first scene and the beginning of the second into blurriness, signaling the progression from dream to reality.

Despite its predictable and sexist conclusion, the film is intriguing. Supposing the British filmmaker, known for his innovations, was the first to have used blur in this way, where did the idea come from? Was this perhaps the result of a productive mistake? Did he realize the potential of cinematographic blur while looking at images he recorded while "messing up" the focus? In any case, the technique, which depends on the progressive transformation of the image, is specifically cinematographic, and it set a precedent: The multiple remakes of *Let Me Dream Again* gave Smith's followers a chance to experiment with fading, in order to suggest the persistence of the dream state after awakening.

Over time, in response to increasing narrative complexity, filmmakers developed a palette of blurs used to signal the moment at which a character loses touch with the objective present and becomes absorbed into dream, hallucination, or memory. With its frequent use of flashbacks, film noir offers some particularly sophisticated examples. If one had to think of only one, the choice might be Richard Fleischer's *Clay Pigeon* (1949). A vision at once pathological and oneiric, this baroque version of losing consciousness combines optical blur and swirling fog (for the beginning and end of the flashback), the denaturation of contrasts (for the remembered episode), and marked effects of rack focus (to designate the return to consciousness).

Similar to film noir, melodrama has always made prominent use of blurred transitions and sequences, less as a means to evoke the resurgence of repressed thoughts or guilty memories, however, than as a reprieve, an escape into dream or memory for characters stuck in desperate daily existences. If such effects, which once gave impressionist cinema and poetic realism their charm, have become rare in contemporary fictional film, it is because mainstream filmmaking practices have banalized them to the point of cliché. Hence, when in *Mommy* (2014) Xavier Dolan returns to classic dream-blur, he plays with the expected dimensions of the effect, wholeheartedly embracing the cliché of soft focus and pathos.

Die is the loving but distraught mother of an unpredictable and excessive teenage boy whom she is trying to keep out of a psychiatric institution. The film's tragic conclusion begins with a waking-dream sequence, the duration of which (more than four minutes) creates unexpected ambiguity and emotional charge. The beginning of the dream and the subjective nature of the images that compose it are clearly signaled by a zoom on Die watching her son, while the first bars of a composition for piano and strings ring out. The following shots, punctuated by slow motion and out-of-focus shots that are increasingly longer and more and more pronounced, deploy all the formulaic elements of the accelerated life-story sequence: graduation, leaving home, a first child, marriage—all of it against a musical backdrop intermixed with scraps of murmured conversation.

Such is the combined affective power of blur, slow motion, and music that it is difficult, even for a viewer aware of this accumulation of visual and audio clichés (Dolan's past experience making television ads is tangible), not to be won over by the lyricism of the images. The longer the sequence lasts, the more the enveloping sweetness of its swirl of blurred images draws us in, and the more we let ourselves hope that this episode is indeed a flashforward and not Die's flight of imagination, her dream of a radiantly normal existence for her son. But the artifice is too apparent, and the end of the sequence is infused with a dull anguish. Faces fade out, melting into nothing more than spots. The murmur of voices becomes an anxious rumble, and the "real" soon resurfaces as the soundtrack returns to sharpness.

The distant relative of the old technique of applying Vaseline to the camera's lens, this kind of blur produces a sense of viscosity that is the opposite of the fleetingness of speed blurs—as if the image itself wished to retain time and the traces of dream and memory, like blotting paper absorbing ink.

Superimposition manifests the same desire to conjure and hold onto that which escapes—dream or nightmare, the loved one or the vampire—but here it occurs via a combination of transparency and sediment. Produced from the simultaneous existence of surplus (several images coexist in the same shot) and lack (the superimposed images are underdeveloped so as to be jointly visible), superimposition is itself a paradox: a visual representation of absence.[1] In its incomplete combination of images, it also provides a striking cinematic demonstration of the "clear versus the confused" that Leibniz associated with waves. Indeed, for expressionist filmmakers, superimposition often helped represent the moving presence of the liquid element. There is the affecting scene in *L'Atalante* (1934), where the heartbroken protagonist plunges into a canal and sees the evanescent shape of his beloved appear there: a small ghost, luminous and smiling, floating in the turbulent water. In *The Faithful Heart*, the desperate lover similarly hallucinates his beloved's face floating in the sea—a nebulous, evanescent image, as impossible to grasp as the transparent waves that trouble the water's surface.

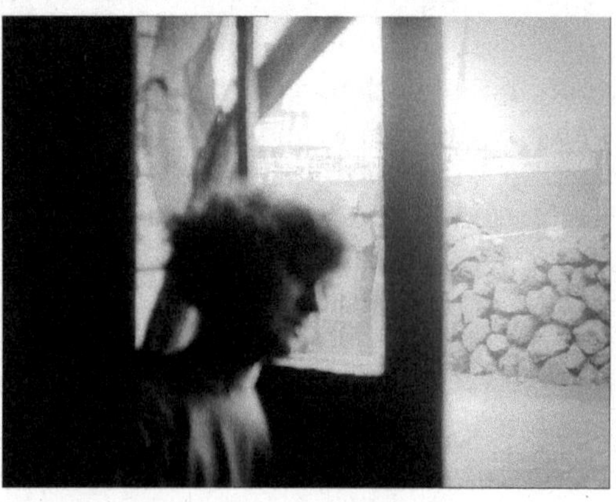

Although in the examples given here, and in the tradition of narrative cinema more generally, blur is a remarkable catalyst for emotion, it remains nevertheless a stylistic convention, a mode of *representing* dreams. The surrealists' ambition was different, since they were not interested in *reproducing* dreams; they wanted to dream in images. Surrealism's program belongs to a particular historical context: It grew out of the rejection of the kind of rationalism that had put technology in the service of destruction and war. Seen this way, the chaotic and confused universes typical of surrealist films represent a sort of nose-thumbing at the technologies of visual precision that made enormous progress during World War I.[2]

For the surrealists, artistic practice was both a method of accessing the unconscious and a means of conjuring it in the conscious visual field. Hence the image, and in particular the photographic image, was valued for its capacity to integrate chance and automatism into the creative process. Yet of all the strategies used in surrealist-inspired cinema, techniques of blur, whose effects cannot be entirely controlled, best show the encounter between contingency and artistic intent that film makes possible.

In the backlash following screenings of Germaine Dulac's film *The Seashell and the Clergyman* (1928), Antonin Artaud criticized Dulac for having treated his script as simply the "reproduction" of a dream. Certainly, in *The Smiling Madame Beudet*, which Dulac made in 1923, the distortions of the image are the result of the characters' imagination: The translucent ghost of the tennis player who appears, thanks to superimposition, to rid Madame Beudet of her execrable husband is clearly indicated as the product of the fed-up wife's fantasy. The oneiric universe of *The Seashell and the Clergyman*, on the other hand, does away with this kind of elucidation. If Dulac draws freely on the techniques of blur characteristic of the avant-gardes of the era, such as smoky superimpositions and other deforming mirrors, the attention paid to effects of light and to the sublimation of matter creates an undeniable kinship with Artaud's project of establishing a dialogue between the material and the spiritual. Vials and flasks sparkle, chandeliers and crystal balls glimmer, and liquid surfaces shine like mirrors. The film works to produce a sort of alchemy of the visible in which the diffraction of light reigns, its sparkle multiplied by dissolves or transformed into haloes by soft-focus techniques.

The difference between *The Seashell and the Clergyman* and Man Ray's film from the same year, *L'étoile de mer* (1928), is striking. To Dulac's shimmering chiaroscuro, Man Ray opposes the nebulous vision of a buried consciousness, deprived of clarity. He opens the film with a shot of a dirty window, using a "mottled or cathedral-glass effect" in the place of blur, and places "pieces of gelatin" on the camera's lens.[3] The result is oppressive, giving the claustrophobic impression of a closed world, as in the image of the titular starfish, kept inside its glass jar.

In both films, however, images succeed to other images according to their own, strange logic. "Issued solely from themselves . . . from a kind of powerful inner necessity," they take shape and disintegrate in atmospheres as unstable as chemical precipitates.[4]

Photogénie of Melancholy[5]

How to represent the "perpetual mobility" of emotion?[6] If the performance of an actor, filmed in sharp focus, can represent emotions precisely (anger, fear, joy: *Emotio* designates an external movement, that which affects me from outside, to which I react), then the blurred image, on the other hand, belongs to the domain of affect, to sentiments that remain indefinite.

To create the indeterminacy of forms and the softness of outlines that allows sense perception to overtake interpretation, many filmmakers work with focus. Some also sometimes employ filters, placed over the camera lens to produce a slightly muddled vision that suggests, variously, intimist painting or a tearful gaze. When the filter affects the whole image, it creates an homogenous softness, pulling the cinematic image toward the painterly; a partial filter, however, creates an exogenous zone at the heart of the image, a place where the uncertain rendering of forms suggests a double spatiotemporal belonging: here, and yet elsewhere.

To abstract oneself from the present in order to better give oneself over to dream: This is the strange state of distraction that Marcel l'Herbier attempts to render through partial blur (the script bears the indication "steam glass mask") in *El Dorado* (1921), a rather conventional exotic melodrama that the filmmaker used as a kind of laboratory of forms. Here blur no longer serves to signal the passage from a waking state to an unconscious one or to intimate that the images are from a dream but to stage "absorption" itself. Working as a metonymy, blur suggests a character so deeply occupied by their thoughts that they seem to partially leave behind the world that surrounds them.[7]

In the film's introductory sequence, we meet Sibilla, a cabaret dancer, waiting to perform on L'Eldorado's stage. Her silhouette is blurry even though the rest of the frame, including her fellow dancers, remains sharp; instead of smiling seductively at the crowd assembled to watch the show, Sibilla sits despondently, thinking of the sick child she left alone to come to work. She is called back to order; the image becomes sharp again.

Commenting on the strangeness of partial blur, Gilles Deleuze speaks of the confusion of "the observer-observed" (the *regardant-regardé*).[8] The camera's gaze does not align with the character's, yet it still demonstrates a particular empathy with her perception and relation to the world. The film does not give us, as we might expect, a confused vision of the cabaret or the crowd attributable to the distracted dancer. Instead, it is Sibilla herself who appears blurry, whose uncertain form seems to hesitate, as if wavering between two places. Blurriness is not the mark of a failure of vision or an expression of a lack of being but, on the contrary, the manifestation of a heightened sensitivity, expressed yet not exposed to view.

Epstein's *The Faithful Heart* contains a comparable sequence in which the filmmaker takes up a cliché from melodrama—the woman pining sadly away at the window—and uses blur to transform and complexify it.

Marie, the film's heroine, is barred from seeing her love and rebuffed by her adoptive parents, the Hochons, proprietors of a café where she is cruelly exploited. She takes refuge near the door and sinks into a melancholic reverie. Epstein films the young woman in a classic medium shot, her face framed by a window. The lens, however, focuses not on Marie but on the exterior space that stretches before the café, with the port in the distance. The slightly misty outline of a boat is silhouetted, sfumato, in the background; it is the stone wall, running through the middle ground, that is in focus. Marie's face appears in profile, backlit and blurred. Contours, contrasts, and textures are soft, from the folds of the young woman's rough smock to the fuzzy crown of her hair and the shadowy areas where the gaze becomes lost. A double effect of sublimation is at work here: the passage from a material body to a vaporous state and the exaltation of the melancholic state. Marie's silhouette softens and becomes more opaque at the same time, as if she were permeable to the murmur of an elsewhere.

In his classic study of Diderot and painting, Michael Fried describes a trend that flourished in the second half of the eighteenth century, a reaction to the theatricality of rococo art: Turning their backs on the spectacular, certain artists strove to represent figures entirely absorbed in thinking, contemplation, or reading. If these scenes of "absorption" seem to exclude the viewer, they nevertheless encourage a different kind of engagement—attentive, empathetic—that in some works stems from their vague or unfinished aspect.[9] This is a different era and a different medium, yet Fried's observations are echoed in the melancholic vision that Epstein gives of his character. The restrained evocation of Marie's overwhelming grief is the opposite of the hysterical theatricality that reigned over the expression of emotions in studio melodramas. Blur evokes a thoughtful sadness and envelops the figure in a protective veil, distancing the dreamer from inquisitive gazes.

In this conflation of the expressive and the protective, Hong Sang-soo's *In Water* (2023) could be a rightful heir to Epstein's, Akerman's, and Antonioni's experiments in filmic blurriness. In effect, if the blurred image, the result of a manipulation of the technical conditions of recording, turns the film into a "*technesthésique*" experience (where our perception is determined by its technical means), then *In Water* stands as a "technesthesia" of melancholia. Its three protagonists, the actress Nam-hee (Kim Seungyun), camera operator Sang-guk (Ha Seongguk), and actor-turned-director Seoung-mo (Shin Seokho), have traveled to Jeju Island, Korea's southernmost territory, to shoot the latter's first film. As with Epstein and Akerman's *The Captive*, the sea is thus an integral part of the film's setting, its presence signaling again the encounter of two regimes of filmic blur: profilmic and focal, natural and technical. Most of *In Water* is shot out of focus, the image turning from defined to blurry without forewarning or narrative rationalization. The focal blur affects the whole of the image. Combined with the crystalline light of the seascape, the result is an impressionistic composition of fuzzy silhouettes caught in a hazy stratum of ground and sky. The palette of warm, subdued tones that infuses the image is interrupted by the occasional splash of bright color (a stack of purple plastic chairs, a shrub with vividly yellow flowers, a fence painted like a color gradient). Though *In Water* offers little more than discreet clues, Seoung-mo's anguish gradually becomes palpable, tingeing the film's atmosphere with a melancholy that eventually appears to touch the two other characters as well. In the indeterminacy of the blurred visual field, the protagonists thus appear to attune themselves to the mood of the island, both a popular tourist destination and a land haunted by a traumatic past.[10] As they walk to the beach at dusk, as through a watercolor painting, the young woman asks the cameraman if he believes in ghosts, thus acknowledging the permeability between the world of the living and the dead that the blurred image helps suggest.[11]

Even in the island's present, not everything can be hidden or sublimated by blur. Though beautifully caught by the film's soft cinematography, like a distant echo of Antonioni's *Red Desert*, the land of *In Water* is disfigured by road works and pollution. An aborted encounter with a woman who cleans the litter left by the tourists on the beach proves decisive, giving the young director the inspiration he seemed to lack and the courage to start shooting. At the very end of the film, Seoung-mo asks his companions to film him as he goes into the sea. Though the fixed shot never leaves his silhouette as he slowly walks deeper in the water, the focal blur makes it impossible to determine whether or not he actually disappears into the sea, leaving us with the confused movement of waves and a mix of seascape noises with the gentle, low-definition sound of a song about heartbreak.

What is it that makes these images so *touching?* Perhaps it is the way they slip, assisted by the imprecision of form, from the legible toward the sensible, the visual toward the tactile (it is perhaps from its affinity with our most deeply buried sense memories, those that precede even speech, that blur draws its affective force).

In the opening credits of *Persona* (1966), Ingmar Bergman sets out to explore this affinity between the touched and the affective that cinematographic blur seems to intimate so powerfully. Here, however, softness is deceptive, and in the famous portrait shots included in the sequence, the female figure's absorption borders cruelly on indifference. The images of the young boy with round glasses caressing a screen on which is displayed the enormous, slightly blurry face of a woman have become emblematic of a modernist cinema that interrogates the foundations of human relationships with surgical precision. The physical and emotional proximity that characterizes the relationship between mother and child is here suggested and at the same time negated (and in the same way, so is the relationship of identification between the viewer and the film's characters). The maternal figure is inaccessible: Sublimated by soft focus photography, she is all soft curves and dim shadow. Yet the surface remains cold and flat: Overlooking the silhouette of the child whose hand trails over her image, she seems indifferent, absorbed, and impenetrable.

The opening credit sequence of Andy Warhol's *Poor Little Rich Girl* (1965) also takes the form of a close-up of a blurred face. Its first images are only decipherable in retrospect: White, rounded forms grazed blurrily by the lens are revealed to be the folded arms of a young woman sleeping (Edie Sedgwick, would-be star and one of Warhol's muses). The camera remains fixed for more than three minutes on her face, which is almost entirely immobile (Sedgwick makes a small movement but does not open her eyes), a milky expanse on whose surface her features are barely sketched.

Affecting the whole of the image, blur creates a double effect of absorption: of the form by the background and of the subject by sleep. In its indefinite rendering, the image evokes proximity, the imprecise sensation of a touch. At the same time, like a veil, blur protects from the gaze, manifesting the model's absorption in a dream state inaccessible to the viewer in a literal way. Then we hear Andy Warhol's voice announcing the film's title; the spell is broken, Sedgwick rises and engages with vague occupations: Ordinary life resurfaces and with it, voyeurism.

In *Poor Little Rich Girl*, blur is the result of a faulty lens or focus. Yet Warhol still used these woolly shots, opioid visions in which Sedgwick's face, prefiguring the "blank generation," resembles a mask. The result of accident rather than expert technological knowledge, the film is the contemporary version—degraded, obscured by the blurriness that affects the whole image—of the "haloed photogenic faces" of silent film, whose deceptiveness Pascal Bonitzer emphasized, claiming that they hid the "fundamental horror" that comes to the surface in Warhol's film.[12]

The Painterly and the Formless

Pictorialism [Joseph Von Sternberg]

A lens shrouded with a scrap of gauze, twice burned by a cigarette, leaving holes through which the director has the shining eyes of the female star appear: From the pictorialist cinema that once dominated Hollywood production in the age of silent film, what comes to mind first are the softened features of actresses' faces, enveloped in luminous haloes, magnified to the point of fetishism by blur—no longer a figure of absorption but the object of fascinated contemplation.

"Soft style," or pictorialist cinematography, is not, however, reducible to this cliché. Filmmakers and photographers belonging to this school shared the project of making their media work not merely to document reality but instead to transform it. This desire to reenchant the world, inspired by painterly models, relied on the methodical denaturation of light, diffracted and molded with the help of frosted lenses, transparent fabrics, or gelatin sheets placed over the lens. Sources of light were brought in and customized, depending on need, as shooting occurred.[1]

Is it because of his interest in both modern and earlier styles of painting that Josef von Sternberg became one of the masters of soft style? Or is it because, before he became a film editor, and then assistant director, he was employed at length in a lace factory, where he learned "the difference between Venetian trimming, Alençon lace, Chantilly, and Valenciennes?"[2] Filters, lights, artificial smoke: Sternberg mastered all techniques but perhaps none better than the use of veils, which he deployed as both internal and external filters.

The final shootout in *Underworld* (1927), the first film Sternberg could claim as entirely his own, contains a sequence in which each effect and each quality of blur is linked to a cinematographic choice—a sequence that unfurls as a sort of soft-style manifesto.

Sought by the police, a gangster takes nighttime refuge in a hiding place that is revealed to be a trap. The parallel montage takes us both out in the street, where the police are pointing a powerful light toward the windows, and inside the apartment, filled with the smoke of heavy gunfire. An incongruous detail appears at the height of the battle: A cat has retreated to the sill of a window fitted with a lace curtain. The fabric filters the light; the background is reduced to the pale reflections of its pattern on the glass. The backlit silhouette of the cat, its fur ruffled, is half hidden by the curtain. A flash of light suddenly illuminates the window: A bullet has just pierced the glass. At the point of impact, a shining rosette appears like an echo of the curtain's embroidered pattern, illuminated by the light from outside. The cat, terrified, jumps away, his shape disappearing into a single blurry streak.

The scene is a study in contrasts: the softness of lines and textures, of the cat's downy fur and the transparent curtains that sift light and shadow in their folds versus the hardness of the window pane, the revolver bullet that shatters it, and the shards of glass that diffract the light.

We find the same richness of contrasts and the same compositional complexity in *The Docks of New York* (1928), filmed two years later. Here, the visual confusion produced by blur inflects the possible interpretations of what the image shows and what it suggests.

Artificial fog and smoke fill the studio set, enshrouding the characters' shapes: Sailors, prostitutes, and other down-and-out figures drift through the port's shady areas, where the story takes place. Bill, the main character, is a stoker employed to fill the coal boilers below the ship's decks. The hold is depicted as a sort of inferno, dark, smoky, sweltering with sexual frustration, a place where the men's bodies appear caged by the shafts of light that filter down from the deck. When Bill, off for the night, leaves the stifling atmosphere of the hold and ventures out onto the quay, he is welcomed by fog and cold—from hell to limbo.

As well as mist and fog, ropes, fences, and nets function as filters internal to the image, with blur eroding the stability of the visual field from the background. A type of composition is thus established that will be repeated in the decor and framing of the sequences that follow: While in the background mist unfurls in gradations of blur, in the foreground an object, or its dark outline, appears clearly delineated. The foreground serves as a sort of gauge, the measure by which human presence, formerly captive of the oppressing and blurry background, becomes more or less tangible.

However, the first appearance of the main female character, Mae, departs from this compositional rule. We do not see the film's heroine, only her deformed reflection, an upside-down shadow materializing gently on the surface of the port's dark waters. The young woman remains immobile for an instant, then straightens up and throws herself into the water. Her body is doubly elided: It appears in the form of a moving shadow, and its fall takes place off screen, only indirectly.[3] We only see its impact—indirect and deferred—on the water's surface.

Worthy of expressionist cinema, this bold initial composition—the oblique line of the quay and, at a right angle with it, the diagonal line of the body extended by the trajectory of the jump —reaches the point of abstraction in the shots that follow the body's plunge into the water. The framing remains unchanged, and the camera stays focused on the dim surface of the water rippling from the impact of the off-screen body.

Bill leaps in to save Mae from drowning, but even then we do not get to see the young woman's face. Hauled back to the quayside, Mae's body lies prone in the middle of a ghostly group of curious onlookers who have emerged from the fog. Sternberg films only her body, covered by a wet dress, shaken by spasms. The images that follow serve to show the heroic act that we have just witnessed in a different, uncertain, light. A quick cut to a close shot of Bill shows him standing slightly apart, observing the scene while getting dressed. The presence of fog, the man's sideways and intense look, the truncated body of the woman, and the slight halo of light that enshrouds the silhouettes: It is a troubling, sick moment in which the erotic and the poignant conjoin.

Several factors contributed to the disappearance of soft-style filmmaking and the rise of sharper cinematography. On the one hand, the changes in contrast and in the degree of blurriness characteristic of soft style worked against the fluidity of montage and presented a problem in the context of an increasingly precise continuity system. (And yet in large part, doesn't the charm of silent cinema's haloed faces come from the way they appear, with no concern for resemblance, between two sequences shot in more "natural" light?)[4] But it is above all the advent of the talking film that led to the end of the pictorialist style of cinematography: a synchronized soundtrack requires a sharp image in which the face's communicative function is paramount.[5] The shift to automatic film development techniques, which homogenized the quality of photography, did the rest.

Working against these trends, however, Sternberg continued to use blur, sometimes in ways that border on abstraction. The distortion present in some of his shots prefigures effects deployed decades later by artists and filmmakers exploring the possibilities of enlargement (including Andy Warhol, Richard Hamilton, Ken Jacobs in *Tom, Tom the Piper's Son* [1969], and of course Antonioni in *Blow-Up*), even to the point of the dissolution of the image's content. Sternberg's use of veils and coverings also has a strange affinity with the video image. Gilles Deleuze cites a striking moment in *The Scarlet Empress* (1934): "In an image that seems to come from video," he writes, the face "is no more than a geometric incrustation of the veil."[6]

The close-up to which Deleuze refers occurs at a key moment in the film, when Marlene Dietrich's character accepts her political destiny. Sternberg films the future empress in bed, surrounded by thick tulle curtains. When a cut turns the medium shot into a close-up, Sternberg sets the focus on the mesh of the tulle. The images of a jubilant crowd (celebrating the birth of a male heir) that soon overlay Dietrich's face appear similarly caught in the fabric's netting. The young woman's features fade to the point of illegibility. It is almost as if the images were the result of refilming a detail from a television screen in extreme close-up, or as if the woven surface that overlays the image had become autonomous, detaching itself from the layer of figuration. In the slow fadeout that concludes the sequence, the shot seems to approach a sort of degree zero of figuration. Dietrich's closed eyes become wells of blackness; her face turns into a mask and, finally, a skull.

In a few images, Sternberg allegorizes the decline of the aura and of the face as object of fascination, the end of a cinema in which "the human face still plunged audiences into the deepest ecstasy, when one literally lost oneself in a human image as one would in a philtre."[7]

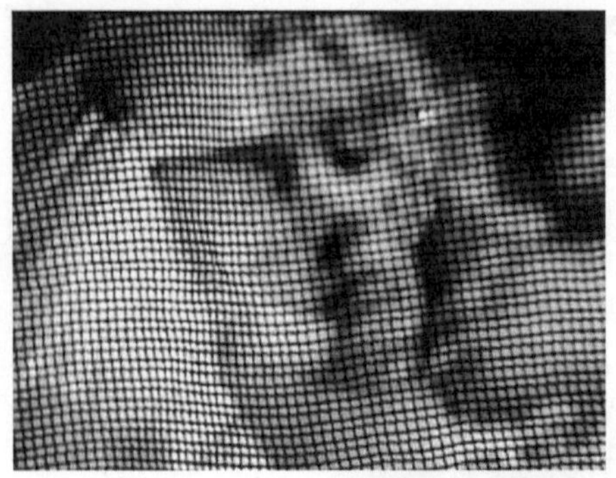

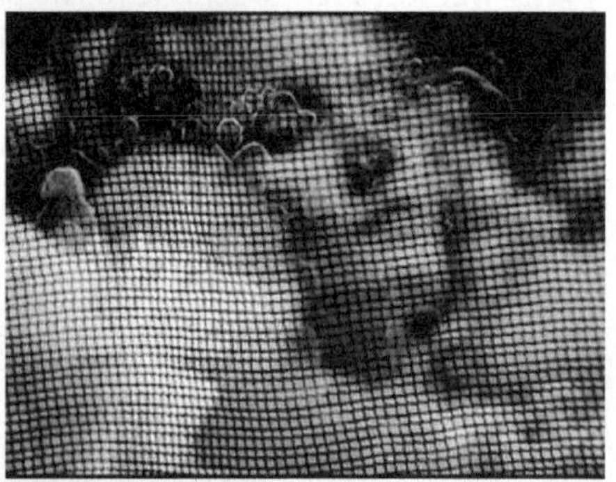

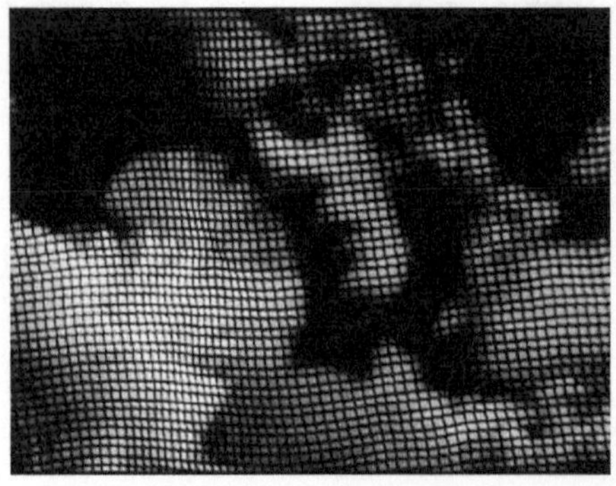

The Appeal of Abstraction
[Michelangelo Antonioni]

The legacy of soft-style cinematography is widespread. The late work of Wong Kar-wai can be seen as its contemporary reincarnation. We also find traces of it in the sfumato treatment of landscapes and the interior chiaroscuros typical of New Hollywood's twilight westerns, films that revisit the myth of the frontier and the American pastoral in light of the violence and misery underlying them. In *McCabe & Mrs. Miller* (Robert Altman, 1971) or *Heaven's Gate* (Michael Cimino, 1980), the softness of the photography has no equal other than the brutality of the worlds that the films depict.[8]

In soft-style cinematography, the quality of the photography works to create a diffuse expressive value—atmosphere, or *Stimmung*—that recalls certain painterly techniques but reminds us also of film's fundamental immateriality, of the projected image's evanescence. Other techniques elicit a more radical fusion of cinema and painting: These extend the presence of blur beyond the simple attenuation of details and play with the plastic qualities of the image to evoke the heft of matter. Alexander Sokurov's work is exemplary of a trend of Russian film that claimed this kind of aesthetic. In *Mother and Son* (1997), for instance, he takes painting as his reference and model, forsaking the sharpness of mainstream cinematography to foreground instead the moving image's capacity to evoke the world in its physicality. The result is a drama of colors, textures, and dramatic lighting in which the human figure is caught.[9]

Similarly interested in the relation of the image to the physical world, the so-called materialist cinema pushed the limits of experimentation. Filmmakers and artists working directly on the film itself—painting, scratching, burying celluloid film—thus continue a rich tradition of cameraless practice that embraces the effect of contingency and its palette of blurs and flirts with abstraction.[10]

Complex expressions of intermedial aesthetics also typified film's second modernity—the period in which Western cinema sought to differentiate itself from the emerging media of television. Whether in the case of slow motion in the explosive final sequence of *Zabriskie Point* (1970), fog in *Identification of a Woman* (1982), the enlargement of the photographic image to the point of its disintegration (*Blow-Up*), or tachist backdrops and focal blur (*Red Desert*), in the work of Michelangelo Antonioni blur extends the plasticity of the image all the way to the point of abstraction.

Flattening of perspective, the separation of forms and colors, the transfiguration of profilmic reality: In *Red Desert*, the blurriest of Antonioni's films, the tendency toward abstraction is palpable, aided by the use of the telephoto lens and the denaturation of colors. This abstraction is distinct from minimalism and its strict, ordered forms; its affinities, instead, lie somewhere between the stains on Leonardo da Vinci's wall and the apparent chaos of art informel. Above all, for Antonioni, the slippage toward the pictorial and toward blur also expresses the anguish of a loss of self.

Red Desert's opening credits, filmed in the industrial port of Ravenna, are as blurry as they are unforgettable: a succession of trembling tableaux, blurred yet precisely framed, somewhere between tachism and a science-fiction setting. The first image is grainy, very blurred, and almost monochromatic. In the lower part of the frame, the tops of a few trees extend their bare branches, faint like sketches in pencil, over a milky expanse of sky. A panoramic movement to the right: a stretch of gray matter, then strange forms cross the frame: the fine, faint shadow of a lamppost, factory smokestacks and blurry colored pipes, and then finally the dark structures of industrial buildings wrapped in clouds of steam.

Blur changes and magnifies the photographic contents of the shots such that the images of *Red Desert*'s credit sequence recall the delicate shadings of Gerhard Richter's "photopaintings." Evoking the embellished, softened vision of some of Richter's landscapes of paint, Juliette Singer compares his canvases to a "poisoned chalice."[11] The expression lends itself well to Antonioni's images: The architectural forms are of course transformed by blur, but the boundaries between air and smoke, form and ground, off- and on-screen space are all porous, letting formlessness seep into the heart of the abstract and industrial poison fill the atmosphere. The beauty of these images is all the more fascinating in that it is rooted in the depiction of an industrial world that is shrouded in softness like a romantic landscape, overlaid by toxic plumes that move with the evanescent grace of innocent clouds.

At the end of the credits, a jet of smoke surges violently from a chimney. Vividly yellow against the pale sky, it has the artificiality and vagueness of the colored shapes that were once stenciled by hand on black-and-white films. Like the red painted flag waving at the top of the mast in *Battleship Potemkin* (1925), the yellow smoke seems to float on the surface of the image. One was a symbol of hope, the other of alienation. And yet, at the foot of *Red Desert*'s factory smokestacks, in the gray, the rain, and the fog, a group of striking workers has gathered.

Toward Formlessness

Of all the film's characters, only Giuliana—and perhaps briefly Corrado, when he daydreams in front of the workers who have come to hear him speak of work and exile and the image blurs—seems capable of opening herself to the world in which she moves.[12] This empathetic sensitivity has a price: the risk that manifests in the way the image tips toward blurriness, giving in to the confusion between the real world and a mental reality, between external sensations and interior turmoil.

In a text that appeared before the advent of abstract art, the art historian Wilhelm Worringer explores the penchant for "abstraction" (understood not in the sense of nonfiguration but in the word's etymological meaning of *abstractus*, to extract or detach) that appears in certain periods of Western art. The desire to "abstract" represented objects from the chaos around them is seen to demonstrate an existential anxiety.[13] Distant, clear, and ordered vision gives us a rational and stable image of the world; blur, on the other hand, demonstrates a powerlessness to hierarchize perceptions or to detach oneself from the world as matter. When the image is homogenized under the effect of wholesale blur, when figure and ground interpenetrate, when the human form, the inanimate, and the organic are all held in the same plane of appearance: This is how the attraction of formlessness, where the subject itself disintegrates, makes itself felt.[14]

This deadly attraction of the formless, already so present in Antonioni's images, today haunts another kind of auteur cinema—one in which experiments with blur provoke an even more radical and more violent confusion between figure and inanimate matter. The impression that chaos hides under the surfaces of things, ready to break through, has perhaps never been as intense as it is now, in the era of the new "frenzy of the visible."

The unbridled circulation of images and sound, the ubiquity of screens and surveillance, the encroachment of the virtual on the real, the labyrinthine accumulation of data and audiovisual archives populated by clones and ghosts: Electronic and digital technologies have added a good dose of strangeness to the world of ubiquitous images. Bucking the trend of high-definition cinematography, forms of blur have multiplied thanks to low-definition formats and processes of reproduction and circulation: digitization, refilming, and other forms of compression. Commercial horror film has made enthusiastic use of these new procedures of recording and circulating images. In its less direct and more reflexive ways, art cinema has also used them to interrogate the strangeness of being in today's world.

From David Lynch to Philippe Grandrieux, from Apichatpong Weerasethakul to Gus Van Sant and Guy Maddin to Harmony Korine, this cinema of sensation builds uncertain, directionless universes open to the murmur of parallel worlds and populated with characters who are no longer able to locate the boundary between their interior vision and what surrounds them. The sloping light of dawns and dusks dominates; the camera focuses with difficulty, and shapes melt into smoggy backgrounds, tangles of rustling undergrowth, or the trembling cross-hatching of urban jungles' neon lights. Bodies seem asynchronous or ill-fitting, either swallowed up or prey to a paroxysmal and painful sensitivity. Often dialogue is lost, engulfed by noises or buzzing static that invades the soundtrack. The shadow of Francis Bacon hovers over the most violent of these universes, in which sensory chaos becomes manifest in the monstrous metamorphosis of bodies.[15]

Some of these filmmakers choose low-definition video for the flux of its ever-changing, terribly empathetic images, which any modification of light or movement of the camera can disrupt. In *Julian Donkey Boy* (1999) or *Inland Empire* (2006), for example, the unsteady camera lens seems incapable of hierarchizing the information that it manages to capture; colors and contours dilute and mix, figure and ground fuse. It is as if both characters and the electronic or digital image were affected by a sort of schizophrenia. In a media context dominated by the obsessive recording of live experiences, this effect is inevitably linked to a logic of the double: the experience of reality through its blurry specter.

Limbo [Gus Van Sant]

Can we conveniently rely on this easy clinical designation, schizophrenia, to lend meaning to the inexplicable and deadly violence depicted in *Elephant* (2003), the most famous and also blurriest of Gus Van Sant's films? Or should we blame stigmatization and bullying, or just the influence of video games on the adolescent psyche? Van Sant scatters clues throughout the film while remaining resolutely vague. The malaise is diffuse, and the sources of harm remain uncertain.

Describing the disenchanted youth who feature in Leos Carax's early films, Serge Daney uses a phrase that just as well describes Van Sant's characters: They are, he says, "not even lost, merely 'added' to the world that surrounds them."[16] In *Boy Meets Girl* (1984) and *Bad Blood* (1986), Carax uses blur poetically, in a way that runs counter to its conventional uses, to suggest the disaffected presence of his characters and their incapacity to communicate with others.

Elephant's signature shot, a long sequence shot in which the camera trails behind high schoolers as they walk down their school's hallways, depicts an even more radical solitude. The lines of flight created by the geometric expanse of the corridors call for a certain depth of field, but the shot's composition forecloses this: While in the foreground, the back of the character's neck is sharp, the rest remains blurred—a point of view lacking both directing lines and perspective.

The film's most chilling sequence takes account of the mysterious and ineluctable nature of the catastrophe by delaying the blurred figure's passage into sharpness all the way to the bottom limit of the frame. The murderer follows two of his victims down the school's deserted hallways. The image is very blurry, and the shape of the killer, who appears backlit at the very end of the hallway, is at first only a splotch. The young man advances without haste toward the camera; the lens does not focus. The ambiance is muted, underwater-like; there's a light buzzing, the noise of a fax machine, birdsong. Suddenly, at the moment it seems close enough to touch, as if in a chemical reaction, the figure of the killer detaches itself from the rest of the image and becomes sharp.

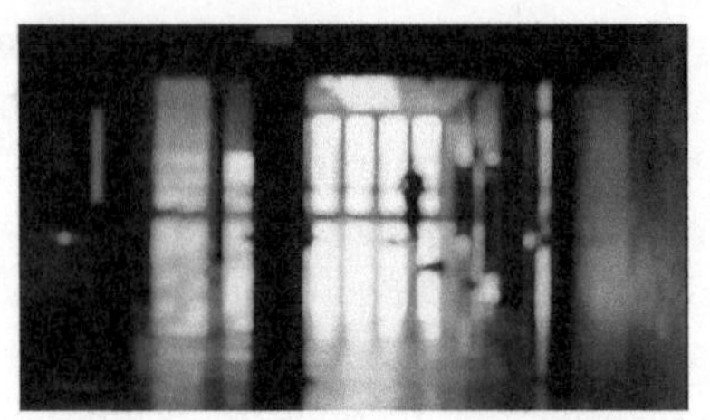

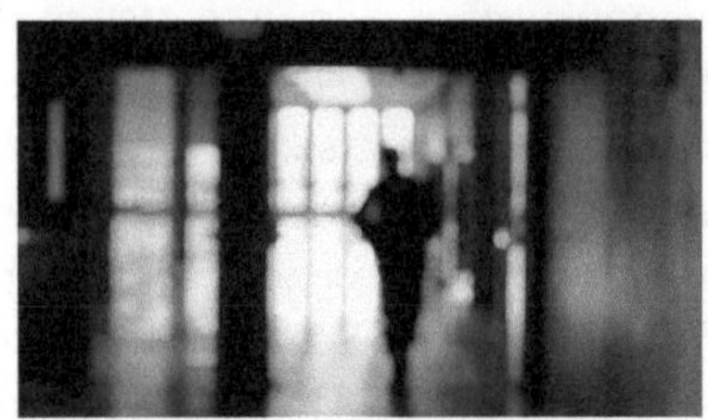

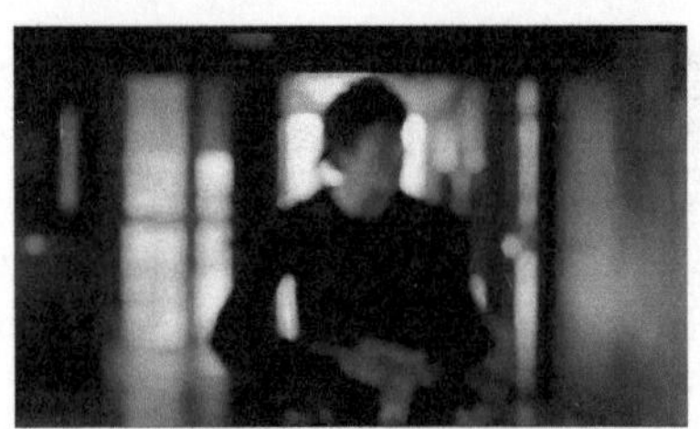

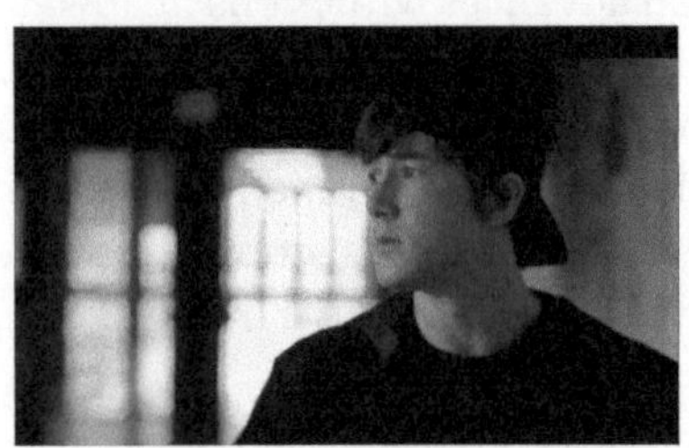

For Van Sant, violence, horror, and death are shrouded in the same softness the director uses to film the beauty of his adolescent actors. The qualities of blur, however, vary from one film to another. *Elephant* unfolds in the circumscribed and aseptic space of a high school. In this minimalist setting, defined by the precise lines of modern architecture, blur is the product of technical effects: blurry focus, absence of depth of field, and slow motion. In *Gerry* (2003), the gaze is sometimes disoriented by mysterious focal blurs, but atmospheric blur dominates, conditioned by the sloping light, the far-off horizons, and the sometimes-uncertain line between earth and sky. In *Last Days* (2005), the environment that the character inhabits is equally determinant. The film follows the last days of a musician who resembles Kurt Cobain, shut away on a vast estate, under the influence of drugs, ignored by a parasitic entourage. Release finally occurs through a sort of shedding, as he leaves his sick, heavy, material body behind. Different effects of blur manifest the different states of the body on screen, between the opacity and organic thickness of matter and the dematerialization and transparent evanescence of the spirit.

At the end of the film, the young man takes refuge in the forest that surrounds the estate, wandering without apparent aim, his failing body swallowed up by the tangle of the undergrowth. The contrast between the confusion and teeming darkness of these shots and the luminous transparency of the images that follow them is striking: Basking in the light of a sunny morning stands an elegant garden pavilion with large bay windows.

A gardener appears in the background and comes forward, collecting his tools. The camera lens, immobile, remains focused on the pavilion, a silent call to the attention of the gardener who, presumably like the majority of the viewers, misses the crucial detail. On the ground, behind the glass door, is an immobile body. The gardener attends to his work, leaving the frame, then reentering the field of vision; this time, he has seen. The first effect of superimposition occurs through a reflection. In the foreground are windows mirroring the surrounding greenery. The interior and the exterior merge so that the body lying inside the building seems to be stretched out on the grass. To this "natural" effect of superimposition is added a ravishingly delicate special effect. A transparent silhouette, naked, rises little by little from the corpse, stands, then climbs the rungs of an invisible ladder before disappearing at the top of the frame.

For the spirit of the young man who died alone to escape and for the magic of the blurred superimposition to operate, the gardener's attentive and presumably benign presence is necessary. Neither intervening nor fleeing, he stands in for the viewer. In these scenes, Van Sant's images recall the beginnings of photography and cinema, the era when these still-new technologies were often used for spiritualist purposes—when film was still, as it were, a "medium." It is no accident if, after the musician's spirit has left the frame, Van Sant depicts his entourage, a group of idle youths, talking before a television screen: Film's spirit world is succeeded by the banal, spectral world of the small screen.

An eminently cinematographic figure, the ghost has long haunted the blurred regions of the screen, thanks to superimpositions, transparencies, or sequences of found footage darkened by the decomposition of the filmstrip.[17] The blurred zone becomes a temporary portal between the worlds of the living and the nonliving—the double of the door that cinema itself opens between the moviegoers gathered in the theater and the ghostly world of the film.

In contemporary genre cinema, interfaces between the world of the living and the dead proliferate with the presence of new technologies. The phantom, having become a simple specter, haunts the internet before progressively infiltrating the space of the living. The filmic image is thus gradually "contaminated" by exogenous images—images from television screens, computers, and surveillance videos—that are distorted by the interference of static or pixelated to the point of abstraction. Between horror film's ectoplasmic apparitions and the more concrete revenants in contemporary fiction films (including Van Sant's, in *Restless* [2011]), there is little place for the old-fashioned ghost with its vague contours, whose diaphanous shape floats around the set. Undoubtedly, these new revenants are more in keeping with the way that the filmic image has transformed with the advent of the digital. Infinitely reproducible, the digital image neither fades nor disappears—it is ageless.

Photogénie of Memory

As it became dematerialized, electronically then digitally, the moving image lost a part of its temporal dimension. This is not only because the filmstrip, like aging skin, bears the marks of the effects of time and repeated projection but also because the history of media is inscribed in the changing nature of its images and its formats: The visual history of the twentieth century unfolds in variations of photographic grain, chromatic tonalities, contrast, and definition. By making temporal distance palpable, the softness of analog photography contributes to giving old films the "aura" that Walter Benjamin considered antithetical to the cinema. By an effect of substitution unique to visual culture's power of suggestion, the image's color, grain, and degree of definition occupy the role of memory in our collective imaginary. Our idea of what life looked like at the beginning of the last century takes the form not of the precise images of a color film in high-definition but rather has the monochromatic aspect and the slight shakiness of films of that era.

Memory and blur are inextricable. Whether as the result of filming conditions or the mark of the passage of time, blur that erases details and contours evokes the way memory operates, with recollection becoming imprecise over time. This does not, however, necessarily diminish the intensity of the memory; to the contrary, troubling the border between vision and the other senses, the blurred image appeals to a multisensory form of memory, inaccurate but no less vivid.

All types of cinema use the changes in the medium's technological support to conjure the past. To insert, in found-footage mode, a sequence of images altered by the passage of time is one of the most widespread techniques for suggesting a bygone era or a memory. If experimental film maintains a deeper relationship with time and memory, this is not simply because experimental forms bypass conventional narrative logics but also because its relationship to time is indissociable from the materiality of the film-object that remains at the heart of its practices.

Characteristic of the creative interest around questions of memory and the archive that has flourished since the 1990s, the filmmaker Martine Rousset's work is part of an experimental tendency that originates in a particular attachment to the material qualities of media and the diversity of its formats. Forgetting, silence, erasure: Rousset claims an aesthetic of the trace and of disappearance to which the palimpsest-like layering of reworked images contributes. In *Chants* (1996), the work of memory is allegorized by a process of rerecording televised documentaries on film. A form of filmed elegy, *Chants* pays homage to the singer Barbara, whose fearful childhood was spent in hiding during the Occupation. Rousset refilms images in 8mm, then in 16mm, retouching the color and manipulating the projection speed through optical printing. The principle of reformatting is here applied in reverse, from electronic media toward photochemical film, the image gaining in materiality as it loses in definition.

The material beauty of *Chants* partakes in the strange seduction of the ruin, lying somewhere between disintegration and sublimation. The singer's shape and face are superimposed over scenes of devastation, then absorbed in fade outs. Contrasted and grainy, the image has the iridescent appearance of old films to which color has been added. The film is blurry because it is "the trace of the trace of the trace."[18] In the place of standardized televisual memory, *Chants* substitutes a filmic memory that is incomplete, imprecise, and auratic: Refilming becomes the principle of a *photogénie* of memory itself.

Rousset's practice is linked to film's photochemical support. But what would twenty-first-century *photogénie* amount to; that is, what would the translation of Epstein's notion to contemporary digital practices be? Could there be a memory of images filmed by cell phone other than the one that exists on a storage card, measured in gigabytes and forgotten immediately upon deletion? Although it was shot using a cell phone, Jean-Charles Fitoussi's *Nocturnes for the King of Rome* (2005) resolutely works against the grain of the hysterical and bulimic habit of live recording encouraged by the ubiquitous presence of tiny cameras. A filmic journal or a sort of memoir from beyond the grave (the narrator, a composer who was born in Italy and returned to die there, never appears on screen), *Nocturnes* slowly unfurls in trembling and delicately blurry shots, punctuated with archival images. Occasionally, a superimposition lets us see the face of the narrator's wife, dead for some time. Ultimately, *Nocturnes* constructs a compendium of pictorial and cinematographic styles spanning media forms and degrees of blur. If the slightly unsteady long takes recall the fragile universe of 8mm film, the film's beach scenes, inundated with light, suggest impressionism. Something of the spirit of the Renaissance also appears in the shimmering chiaroscuro of the nocturnal sequences and the rounded softness of faces captured in close-up. Rather than in HD or 3D, is it not through low definition, in the uncertain territory of grainy images like these, that the plastic richness and the historical sensibility of the digital image can be found?

Technology Has No Rules

In the beginning, technology has no rules. Then we teach it how to speak.

—Jean-Luc Godard

Isn't the indistinct [picture] often exactly what we need?

—Ludwig Wittgenstein

In the transitional period in which cinema finds itself in the first quarter of the twenty-first century, the coexistence of multiple technical supports gives rise to an unparalleled richness of formal possibilities.[1] Different formats and types of photochemical film have habituated the viewer to diverse patterns of emulsion or film grain and the resulting variability of the softness of outlines and contrasts: Electronic images (with their interlacing, retouching, and afterimage effects) and then digital images (in low definition or, conversely, in high definition and with special effects, or with glitch and datamoshing, which have all generated their own particular effects of blur).[2] Moreover, adding a little "noise" to standard imaging, digital formats can also simulate the vibration, the grain, and the changeability of photochemical blur.

But the growth of these technological capacities also tends, paradoxically, to lead to an impoverishment of cinematic language. Cameras are no longer simple machines but computers: Automatic focus becomes the norm, and the role of chance and invention decreases accordingly.

The philosopher Vilém Flusser argued that the first task of the artist as photographer or filmmaker consists in resisting the temptations of automation and setting oneself apart from the simple machine operator.[3] Agnès Varda takes on this principle in *The Gleaners and I* (2000), when, in a pastiche of a television ad, she dissects the instruction manual of a small digital camera. These devices, she muses, are "marvelous": A mere pull-down menu gives access to "stroboscopic effects, narcissistic effects, and even hyper-realistic effects." Adding action to her words, Varda films and lets herself be filmed, taking inventory of a whole panoply of blurs as she does, from the colored soup of a moving shot recorded in slow motion to the pixelized chaos of datamoshing. Finally, the camera's fluttering gaze alights on the filmmaker's hand. One hand films the other: Technology is nothing without the filming subject.

Goodbye to Language (2014): The title expresses the same desire for the unfettered use of technology as the playful instruction manual sequence in *The Gleaners and I*. In this film, Godard sets in motion all the possibilities of the digital image: He shoots in 3D, with smartphones and Go-Pro cameras as well as regular cameras, sliding the image toward painting or even video art. Blur is everywhere, in all its forms: in the vacillation of dissociating outlines, the dazzling saturation of colors, the crisscrossing of headlights on a road at night, in the rippling surface of a lake, in the wavering reflection of trees on the surface of a river, in sonic overlap and layering, in the disjunction of the image under the effects of 3D.

In this film, 3D is employed not to create the illusion of a homogeneous three-dimensional space—Godard does film with several cameras, but these are imperfectly aligned—but instead to expose the gaps, disorienting the eye, pulling it beyond its comfort zone. In the scenes that feature couples, blurred cinematography depicts the male-female relation as a form of heterogeneity, marked by a gap. In such scenes, the 3D images tend to fall apart: The spectator has to choose between the two figures, between what the left eye sees and what the right eye sees—to see the woman or to see the man, until the images fuse together once more. There is no longer one point of view but several, whose imperfect convergence produces a shifting, blurred vision. But Godard also films children and a dog, and in those sequences, the unstable and shaky image appears to take account of a world in which "we [adult men and women] are not alone."[4]

For Godard as for Varda, image technology is not meant to sustain the expression of a consuming gaze or of certainty of thought. It does not serve to eradicate the effects of chance or to eliminate the indefinite part of the cinematographic image. Neither is it a question of replacing a regime of the (sharp) image with another (blurred) that would be artificially opposed to it. What matters is to preserve the spaces where the eye might escape automation and its induced habits and to doubt, to wander instead. Blur will always be the indispensable ally of a cinema that explores the "ambiguous" relationship between "beings who are both embodied and limited and an enigmatic world."[5]

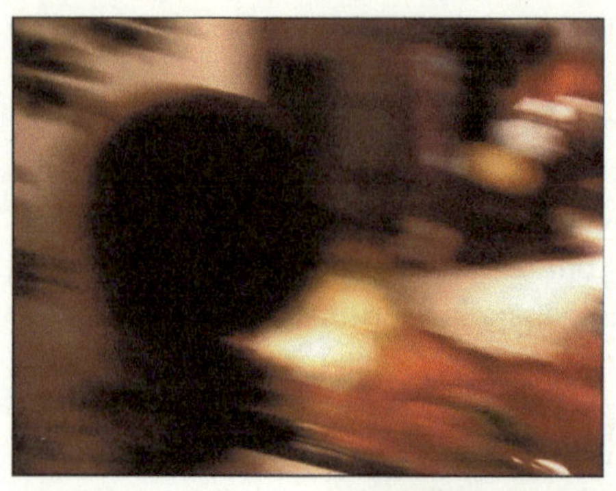

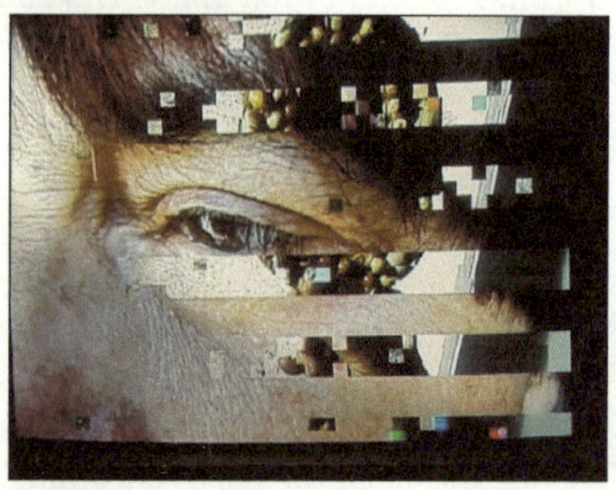

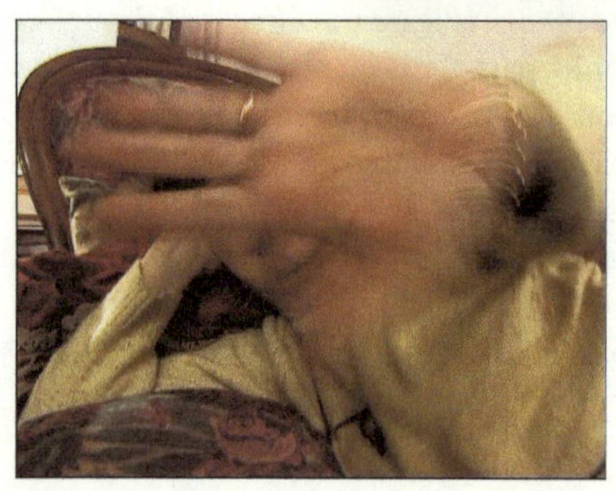

Notes

Prologue (Myopia)

1   Epigraphs: Dominique Chateau, "Les limites du flou," in *Vagues figures, ou, Les promesses du flou* (Publications de l'Université de Pau, 1999), 46; Stan Brakhage, *Metaphors on Vision* (1963; Anthology Film Archives and Light Industry, 2017), 29.

 From *Spellbound* (Alfred Hitchcock, 1945) to *Delicatessen* (Marc Caro and Jean-Pierre Jeunet, 1991) to *Snake Eyes* (Brian De Palma, 1998), female nearsightedness has been the source of numerous suspenseful or comedic scenes. In classical and commercial film, wearing glasses is usually the sign of repressed female desire or of a curiosity and knowledge that threatens the established order. The myopic female character must thus remove her glasses (and become desirable and vulnerable) or risk being marginalized, even eliminated. In *Strangers on a Train* (Alfred Hitchcock, 1951), for example, the killing of Miriam—a wife cast as a character as despicable as she is myopic—is reflected in her glasses, which have fallen during the struggle with her murderer.

2   The cinematographer Otto Heller made the unusual choice to use the techniscope, which lent itself to the use of wide-angle lenses even indoors and in low light.

3   Alain Tanner on the use of Super 8 in his film *In the White City* (1983), in the bonus material from the MK2 Vidéo DVD, 2007.

In Praise of Indistinction

1   André Bazin, "William Wyler, or the Jansenist of Directing," in *Bazin at Work*, trans. Alain Piette and Bert Cardullo (Routledge, 1997), 8.

2   This phenomenon occurs several times in the film, through similar camera movements that are accompanied by reframing.

3   Arthur Wheelock, *Perspective, Optics, and Delft Artists Around 1650* (Garland, 1977), 298.

4   "Je vous aime" or "Je vous aime bien" ("I love you," "I like you"): The jealous lover tries to understand the nature of the slightly murky relationship between the two women. The scene is also reminiscent of Georges Demeny's cinematographic self-portrait, a lip-reading exercise entitled *Je vous aime* (1891).

5   For Gilles Deleuze and Félix Guattari, Proust's Albertine and her group of friends are an example of the fluctuating forms of identity ("becoming"). Gilles Deleuze and Félix Guattari, *A Thousand Plateaus*, trans. Brian Massumi (University of Minnesota Press, 1987), 36.

6   Akerman's Simon is both conscious of the destructive character of his obsession and incapable of resisting it; he wants to know, but he dreads the end of the mystery, which will also mean the end of love and desire. As a consequence, he can approach Ariane's body only when she's asleep or inaccessible, as in the shower scene, in which a frosted glass separates him from the young woman, whose silhouette, distorted by the uneven panes, is impossible to make out distinctly.

7   Daniel Arasse, *Vermeer: Faith in Painting*, trans. Terry Grabar (Princeton University Press, 1996), 74.

8   Translator's note: the homonymic play is mostly lost in English, since I have mainly translated the adjective *vague* as "indistinct," preferring to emphasize the physical manifestation of this quality.

9   Italo Calvino's character Mr. Palomar has a frustrating experience of this phenomenon in "Reading a Wave," a markedly filmic literary text. Italo Calvino, *Mr. Palomar*, trans. William Weaver (Harvest, 1986). With *The Wave* (HD video, 2009), on the contrary, the artist Peter Campus embraces the wave's elusive and painterly nature, experimenting with the pixilation of video such that the image begins to resemble a moving painting.

10 On waves/the vague and poetic inspiration, see Georges Didi-Huberman, "Aesthetic Immanence," in *Dynamics and Performativity of Imagination: The Image Between the Visible and the Invisible*, ed. Bernd Huppauf and Christoph Wulf (Routledge, 2009), 49–50.

11 Gottfried Wilhelm Leibniz, *New Essays Concerning Human Understanding*, trans. Alfred Gideon Langley (MacMillan, 1896), preface, 48.

12 In Étienne-Jules Marey's first chronophotographic film, *La vague* (1891), the movements of the sea crashing against a rock are lost in the swirl of the foam (the scientist was apparently uninterested in screening these images for the public).

13 Henri de Parville, "Le cinématographe," *Les Annales Politique et Littéraires*, April 26, 1896.

14 Jean-Louis Comolli coined the expression to describe the multiplication and omnipresence of images in the second half of the nineteenth century, a first "visual turn" reprised and intensified by the advent of the digital era. Jean-Louis Comolli, *Cinema Against Spectacle: Technique and Ideology Revisited* (Amsterdam University Press, 2015), 284.

15 This "fuzzy logic" starts from the principle that the truth cannot be "of the order of 0 or 1" but exists somewhere between the two. Martin Jay, "Genres of Blur," *Common Knowledge* 18, no. 2 (Spring 2012): 225. See also Bernd Huppauf, "Between Imitation and Simulation: Towards an Aesthetics of Fuzzy Images," in *Dynamics and Performativity of Imagination: The Image Between the Visible and the Invisible*, ed. Bernd Huppauf and Christoph Wulf (Routledge, 2009), 231.

16 See Leonardo da Vinci's "Treatise on Painting," as well as E. H. Gombrich's *Art and Illusion: A Study in the Psychology of Pictorial Representation* (Princeton University Press, 1960), in which Gombrich evokes "the beholder's share," or the viewer's active participation in the interpretation and conceptualization of the work, which is not immediately "readable."

17 Gaston Bachelard, *On Poetic Imagination and Reverie*, trans. Colette Gaudin (Bobbs-Merrill, 1971), 19–20.

18 Daniel Arasse, *Leonardo da Vinci: The Rhythm of the World*, Rosetta Translations (Konecky & Konecky, 1998), 271.

19 David Bordwell, Janet Staiger, and Kristin Thompson, *The Classical Hollywood Cinema: Film Style and Mode of Production to 1960* (Routledge, 1985), 292.

20 Paul Virilio, *War and Cinema: Logistics of Perception*, trans. Patrick Camiller (Verso, 1989), 70.

21 The term was first coined by the artist Harun Farocki, "Phantom Images," *Public* 29 (2004): 17.

22 As Trevor Paglen summarizes: "We've long known that images can kill. What's new is that nowadays, they have their fingers on the trigger." Trevor Paglen, "Operational Images," *E-Flux* 59 (2014), https://www.e-flux.com/journal/59/61130/operational-images/.

23 Although it applies to the field of the arts, Georges Didi-Huberman's critique of the "tone of certainty" adopted by experts resonates with the kind of discourses generated in domains of activity where operational images are produced and circulated. George Didi-Huberman, *Confronting Images: Questioning the Ends of a Certain History of Art*, trans. John Goodman (Penn State University Press, 2005), 2–4.

24 Such footage can be found on various web platforms generally accessible to the public at large, including on YouTube. Éléonore Weber's approach thus aligns with that of investigative journalists who rely on open-source intelligence (Osint) for part or all of their sources. See Jean-Paul Fourmentraux, "Dans l'oeil du viseur: vision armée, images opératoires et contre-visualités. Autour du film d'Éléonore Weber, Il n'y aura plus de nuit (2020)," *Sociétés & Représentations* 1, no. 55 (2023): 101.

25 An expression coined by the artist Hito Steyerl in the manifesto in which she famously hails the radical potential of digitized material that has deteriorated through successive compressions and the vicissitudes of image circulation and sharing. Hito Steyerl, "In Defense of the Poor Image," *E-Flux Journal* 10 (2009).

26 Jean Epstein, *Écrits sur le cinéma*, tome 2 (Seghers, 1975), 18 ; Jean Epstein, *L'intelligence d'une machine* (Jacques Melot, 1946), 48.

27 Didi-Huberman, *Confronting Images*. See also Agamben's reading of Aristotle in Giorgio Agamben, *Potentialities: Collected Essays in Philosophy* (Stanford University Press, 2000), 183–85.

Definition

1 Pascal Martin speaks of a "continuum" between blurriness and sharpness. Pascal Martin, "Transition," in *Les frontières du flou au cinéma*, ed. Pascal Martin and François Soulages (L'Harmattan, 2014), 5–7, 205.

On the technical and creative aspects of blur in film, see also the work of Bidhan Jacobs.

2   Jean-Baptiste Thoret, *26 secondes, l'Amérique éclaboussée: l'assassinat de JFK et le cinéma américain* (Rouge Profond, 2003).

Aesthetics of Blur

1   Prosper Hillairet, *Coeur fidèle* (Yellow Now "Côté films," 2008). The terminology is slightly imprecise: Technically in the Lumière brothers' film, blur is motion blur. Shakiness, as in the shaky camera effect, generally indicates blur that is the result of the movement of the camera itself.

2   Siegfried Kracauer, *Theory of Film: The Redemption of Physical Reality*, trans. Miriam Bratu Hansen (Princeton University Press, 1997), 89.

3   Germaine Dulac, *Writings on Cinema (1919–1937)*, trans. Scott Hammen, ed. Prosper Hillairet (Paris Experimental, 2018), n.p.

Rain, Mist, Fog

1   Josef von Sternberg, who makes frequent use of cigarette smoke in his films, mentions the smoke-filled air of movie theaters in his memoirs. Josef von Sternberg, *Fun in a Chinese Laundry* (Collier, 1973). More recently, the artist Anthony McCall has emphasized the importance of the presence of dust and cigarette smoke in his projector-based works. Crucial to the initial projections of *Line Describing a Cone* (1973) in movie theaters, these elements were soon replaced by a smoke machine, a reminder of Etienne-Jules Marey's early experimentations. Anthony McCall, "Line Describing a Cone and Other Films," in *Experimental Film and Video: An Anthology*, ed. Jackie Hatfield (John Libbey, 2006), 64.

2   Siegfried Kracauer, *Theory of Film: The Redemption of Physical Reality*, trans. Miriam Bratu Hansen (Princeton University Press, 1997), li.

3   Gilles Deleuze uses the term "crystalline regime" to describe this sort of image.

4   In *The Monadology*, Leibniz evokes the multiplicity of points of view that contribute to our perception of a town that "looked at from various sides, appears quite different." Gottfried Wilhelm Leibniz,

The Monadology and Other Philosophical Writings, trans. Robert Latta (Oxford University Press, 1898), 248.

Focus

1   Raymond Bellour, *Between-the-Images*, trans. Allyn Hardyck (Les Presses du Réel, 2012), 100.

2   Germaine Dulac, *Writings on Cinema (1919–1937)*, trans. Scott Hammen, ed. Prosper Hillairet (Paris Experimental, 2018), n.p.

3   Blur is thus part of what Jacques Aumont calls the filmic image's "power of apparition." Jacques Aumont, "Le cinema, un art d'apparition," in *Que peut une image?* (Le Bal Textuel–Centre National des arts plastiques: Les Carnets du Bal, 2014), 88–106.

4   Except when it is revealed by radically slowing down the image, as in the artist Douglas Gordon's installation 24 *Hour Psycho*, 1993. See also the analysis of "psychotropics" by Nicole Brenez, in *On the Figure in General and the Body in Particular*, trans. Ted Fendt (Anthem, 2023), 158–61.

5   The video artist and filmmaker Johan Grimonprez includes this television sequence in his essay film on Hitchcock and the double, *Double Take* (2010). Blur is used to numerous effects in *Double Take*, which opens with a shot of fog that is itself doubled: The natural fog is overlaid by television static. See also Serge Daney's observations on the television image, reproduced with commentary by Caroline Chik in *L'image paradoxale. Fixité et movement* (Presses du Septentrion, 2011), 150.

6   Maurice Merleau-Ponty, *Phenomenology of Perception*, trans. Colin Smith (Routledge, 2002), 176.

7   "To touch is to touch a limit, a surface, a border, an outline. Even if one touches an inside, 'inside' of anything whatsoever, one does it following the point, the line or surface, the borderline of a spatiality exposed to the outside, offered—precisely—on its running border, offered to contact." Jacques Derrida, *On Touching, Jean-Luc Nancy*, trans. Christine Irizarry (Stanford University Press, 2005), 103.

8   In the case of Woody Allen's film, the actor's shape is cut out and replaced, image by image, with its blurred double. See Giusy Pisano's

prologue in *Les frontières du flou au cinéma*, ed. Pascal Martin and François Soulages (L'Harmattan, 2014).

9   Defamiliarization here is meant in the sense proposed by Victor Shklovsky in *Art as Technique* (1917).

Motion Blur

1   The manual for the Lumière brothers' cinématographe indicates the best possible position for the shutter in cases where the user wishes to capture blurry images—for reproducing "very rapid movements for which the blur of images further contributes to increasing the illusion as sharper images would not, since in such cases these would produce a jerky recomposition of movement." Auguste Lumière and Louis Lumière, technical sheet and user's manual for their cinematograph, published in *La Revue du Siècle*, May–June 1897.

2   Philippe Dubois, Marc-Emmanuel Mélon, and Colette Dubois, "Cinéma et Vidéo: interpénétrations," *Communications* 48 (1998): 273, 276.

3   In modern forms of transportation, the closer the passing landscape, the blurrier it appears; speed deprives us of the foreground. See Enda Duffy, *The Speed Handbook: Velocity, Pleasure, Modernity* (Duke University Press, 2009), 175; as well as Christa Blümlinger, *Cinéma de seconde main. Esthétique du remploi dans l'art du film et des nouveaux médias* (Klinksieck "Collection d'ésthétique," 2013), 88.

4   See Barbara Turquier, "La rédemption de la ville: *New York* et le cinéma underground américain (1962–1975)," doctoral thesis, Paris 7 Diderot, 2013.

5   Like the time-lapse technique, slit-scan is based on the capture of movement image by image over a long exposure time but is distinguished, in its initial mechanical form, by a more complex setup: The camera films colored patterns placed behind an opaque mask pierced with slits, hence the distinct trails of light it produces. Interestingly, one of the inspirations for Trumbull's technique was the work of John Whitney, notably on the credit sequence for Alfred Hitchcock's *Vertigo* (1958).

6   Kriss Ravetto, "Bill Viola and the Cinema of Indefinite Bodily Experience," in *Indefinite Visions: Cinema and the Attraction of*

Uncertainty, ed. Martine Beugnet et al. (Edinburgh University Press, 2017), 223–41.

7 Raymond Bellour, *Between-the-Images*, trans. Allyn Hardyck (Les Presses du Réel, 2012), 119, which remains the principal work on Godard's slow motion.

8 Bellour uses the word *concrétude* to describe the moments of fragile equilibrium that happen at the heart of a blurred sequence, when matter and form seem to coincide suddenly. Raymond Bellour, *Le corps du cinéma* (P.O.L., 2009), 351.

9 In "On Potentiality," Giorgio Agamben reconsiders Aristotle's line of thinking, attempting to transcend the dualist conception by which potential is only the substrate of the actual (to paraphrase his argument, we can say that just as darkness exists in itself and not only as the negative of lightness, blur exists as itself and not only as the negative of the defined). The conclusion of his thinking recalls Godard's images. Agamben brings the notion of potentiality together with the exercise of freedom in one of his most fundamental expressions: The freedom embodied in potentiality is the freedom not to be defined. Giorgio Agamben, *Potentialities: Collected Essays in Philosophy* (Stanford University Press, 1999), 183–85.

10 Pascal Bonitzer describes *Every Man for Himself* as a chilling film that "leaves no room for the slightest uncertainty, the slightest shaky line." Pascal Bonitzer, "Peur et commerce," *Cahiers du Cinéma* 316 (October 1980): 6.

11 Excerpt from the character Denise's internal monologue.

12 To film *Napoléon*, Gance employed a small Debrie camera, manipulable and resistant, that his technician adapted to the film's triple shots.

13 See Laurent Jullier, "Dis-moi ce que tu vois: Le régime visuel du *run and gun*," *Mise au Point* 5 (2013), http://map.revues.org/1371.

14 Béla Balázs, *Béla Balázs: Early Film Theory (Visible Man and The Spirit of Film)* (Berghahn, 2010), 156.

15 Jon Jost, "Leighton Pierce: Master Miniaturist," *Senses of Cinema*, May 2022, http://sensesofcinema.com/2002/feature-articles/pierce.

16 This is all the more the case given that cinema actually establishes a double distance: between the camera and its object and between

the viewer and the screen. But this distance should be qualified: To see is to exercise a power of ubiquity, to be both in the spot from which we see and to project ourselves toward what we see. In *The Visible and the Invisible* (1964), Merleau-Ponty lingers over the motif of intertwining as the ultimate exemplification of the reversibility (between toucher and touched, between self and other) inherent in the connection between touching and seeing.

17 "It is because the body of the other does not allow itself to be fixed, determined, that it can be thought of as the place where the endlessness of freedom can express itself." Isabelle Thomas-Fogiel, "Figure et défiguration: la problématique du sublime," in *Vagues figures, ou, Les promesses du flou* (Publications de l'Université de Pau, 1999), 39.

Reveries of the Image

1   Marc Vernet, *Figures de l'absence. De l'invisible au cinéma* (Cahiers du Cinéma, 1998).

2   Paul Virilio, *War and Cinema: The Logistics of Perception* (Verso, 1989).

3   Man Ray, *Self Portrait* (Little, Brown, 1999), 225.

4   Antonin Artaud, "Cinema and Reality," in *Selected Writings* (Farrar, Straus and Giroux, 1976), 151.

5   One way to define the multifaceted concept of *photogénie* is as an attempt to describe cinema's unique capacity to account for human reality as a reality in a state of becoming. *Jean Epstein: Critical Essays and New Translations*, ed. Sarah Keller and Jason N. Paul (Amsterdam University Press, 2012), includes discussions of Jean Epstein's theorizations of *photogénie*, as well as a translation of the texts in which he attempts to conceptualize the relationship of cinema to movement and time. See, in particular, Éric Bullot, "Thoughts on *Photogénie Plastique*," 245–65. See also Muriel Pic, *W. G. Sebald—L'image papillon (suivi de W. G. Sebald: L'art de voler)* (Presses du Réel, 2009). Epstein's own filmmaking, as we have seen, makes extensive use of blur.

6   Jean Epstein, *Écrits sur le cinéma* (Club-Seghers, 1975), 2:18.

7   Michael Fried, *Absorption and Theatricality: Painting and the Beholder in the Age of Diderot* (University of California Press, 1980).

8   Gilles Deleuze, *Cinema 1: The Movement-Image*, trans. Hugh Tomlinson and Barbara Habberjam (University of Minnesota Press, 2003), 71.
9   Fried, *Absorption and Theatricality*. This is, of course, at odds with the blurring of faces for reasons of privacy protection, to which contemporary media and the internet's tools of spatial navigation have accustomed us as a response to techniques of surveillance and control.
10 Ten percent of the population of Jeju Island was massacred as part of the repression of the Jeju uprising of 1948.
11 The line of dialogue echoes the famous exchange between Bulle Ogier and Jacques Derrida in Ken McMullen's *Ghost Dance* (1983).
12 Pascal Bonitzer, *Peinture et cinéma. Décadrages* (Cahiers du Cinéma, 1985), 90. Warhol's work, as Laura Mulvey points out, associates the strategies of unveiling characteristic of modernism with "the topography of feminine surface and its underside, which suggests death and decay." Laura Mulvey, "Some Thoughts on Theories of Fetishism in the Context of Contemporary Culture," *October* 65 (1993): 14.

The Painterly and the Formless

1   "Soft style" is the term used in the United States, where this cinematic style was established. David Bordwell, Janet Staiger, and Kristin Thompson give a description that details its properties in *The Classical Hollywood Cinema: Film Style and Mode of Production to 1960* (Routledge, 1985), 288–92.
2   Josef von Sternberg, *Fun in a Chinese Laundry* (Collier, 1973), 17.
3   From *The Reflecting Pool* (1979) to *Ocean Without a Shore* (2007) and *Three Women* (2008), we could make an inventory of Bill Viola's video work that echoes this scene, using video technology to similarly deconstruct the figure's mode of appearing and disappearing.
4   Bordwell, Staiger, and Thompson, *The Classical Hollywood Cinema*, 292.
5   Bordwell, Staiger, and Thompson, *The Classical Hollywood Cinema*, 288–92.
6   Gilles Deleuze, *Cinema 1: The Movement-Image*, trans. Hugh Tomlinson and Barbara Habberjam (University of Minnesota Press, 1987),

93. See also Mary Ann Doane, *Femmes Fatales: Feminism, Film Theory, Psychoanalysis* (Routledge, 1991), 73.

7   Roland Barthes, *Mythologies*, trans. Annette Lavers (Farrar, Straus and Giroux, 1972), 56. In 1950, in *Sunset Boulevard*, Billy Wilder would once again turn to the close-up on the face, using a combination of blur and fade to put the final touches to his cruel portrait of a fallen movie star—a shot emblematic of a process of disenchantment that drove the sublimating, auratic uses of blur to obsolescence.

8   Emmanuelle Delanoé-Brun, "American Pastorals: Horizons et origines imaginaires dans *Days of Heaven, Heaven's Gate*, et *Matewan*," *Revue d'Études Américaines* 142 (2015): 107–21.

9   Ágnes Pethő, ed., *Caught In-Between: Intermediality in Contemporary Eastern European and Russian Cinema* (Edinburgh University Press, 2021).

10 Kim Knowles, "(Re)visioning Celluloid: Aesthetics of Contact in Materialist Film," in *Indefinite Visions: Cinema and the Attraction of Uncertainty*, ed. Martine Beugnet et al. (Edinburgh University Press, 2017), 257–73.

11 *Collection art contemporain. La collection du Centre Pompidou, Musée national d'art moderne* [catalog], ed. Sophie Duplaix (Centre Pompidou, 2007).

12 This heightened sensitivity is perhaps shared by both director and his character; blur, the mark of the fusion between the director's vision and his character's, is part of what Pier Paolo Pasolini would call free indirect style.

13 Wilhelm Worringer, *Abstraction and Empathy: A Contribution to the Psychology of Style*, trans. Michael Bullock (Ivan R. Dee, 1997).

14 "Affirming that the universe resembles nothing and is only formless amounts to saying that the universe is something like a spider or spit." George Bataille, "Informe," in *Documents* 7 (December 1929): 382. Cited in and see also Yve-Alain Bois and Rosalind Krauss, *Formless: A User's Guide* (Zone, 1997), 18.

15 In his study of Bacon's painting, Gilles Deleuze observes, "It is the same body which, being both subject and object, gives and receives the sensation. . . . This is why sensation is the master of deformations,

the agent of bodily deformations." Gilles Deleuze, *Francis Bacon: The Logic of Sensation*, trans. Daniel W. Smith (Continuum, 2003), 35–36.

16 Serge Daney, "Carax, première fois," *Libération*, May 17, 1984. English translation: http://sergedaney.blogspot.com/2021/05/cannes-1984-leos-carax-first-time.html.

17 Muriel Pic describes the effect of blur as a way of "photographing ghostliness." Muriel Pic, *W. G. Sebald—L'image papillon (suivi de W. G. Sebald: L'art de voler)* (Presses du Réel, 2009), 163.

18 *Martine Rousset*, documentary by Michel Amarger and Frédérique Devaux (Re:voir Vidéo, 2000). See also *Jeune, pure, et dure. Cent ans de cinéma expérimental*, ed. Nicole Brenez and Christian Lebrat (Cinémathèque Française, 2005), 520.

Technology Has No Rules

1   Epigraphs: Jean-Luc Godard, interview, 2014, http://cpn.canoneurope.com/content/Jean-Luc_Godard.do; Ludwig Wittgenstein, *Philosophical Investigations*, trans. G. E. M. Anscombe (Macmillan, 1953), section 71, p. 34.

Jean-Pierre Beauviala describes this transitional period as a "baroque" one: "We choose a format, a means of recording, according to what we want to see appear on the screen. It is one of those rare periods—perhaps the only—in which we have such colossal choice." Benjamin Bergery, Diane Baratier, and Caroline Champetier, "L'avenir de l'image cinématographique. Entretien avec Jean-Pierre Beauviala," *Lumières: Les Cahiers AFC* 1 (2006): 85–101.

2   In such manipulation of the video compression process, key frames containing the information or the pixels necessary to recreate the full image are deleted. The mixing of pixel blocks across incomplete frames results in a sort of disordered mosaic, giving the impression of several images competing to emerge simultaneously. See especially the work of Jacques Perconte and Nicolas Provost.

3   Vilém Flusser, *Towards a Philosophy of Photography*, trans. Anthony Mathews (Reaktion, 2000).

4   Maurice Merleau-Ponty, *The World of Perception*, trans. Oliver Davis (Routledge, 2004), 70.

5   Merleau-Ponty, *The World of Perception*, 70.

Figures

Martine Beugnet is Professor in Visual Studies at the Université Paris Cité and a member of ECHELLES, a CNRS research institute. In English, she is the author of *Cinema and Sensation* (2007, 2012) and *Claire Denis* (2004), coauthor of *Proust at the Movies* (2005), and coeditor of *Indefinite Visions: Cinema and the Attractions of Uncertainty* (2017).

Lindsay Turner is Associate Professor of English and Creative Writing at Case Western Reserve University. She is the author of two collections of poetry and has translated books by Stéphane Bouquet, Éric Baratay, Souleymane Bachir Diagne, Anne Dufourmantelle, Richard Rechtman, Ryoko Sekiguchi, and others.

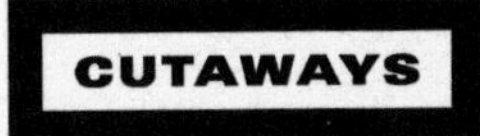

SERIES EDITORS:
Erika Balsom and **Genevieve Yue**

Elena Gorfinkel, John David Rhodes, *The Prop*

Jules O'Dwyer, *Hotels*

Martine Beugnet (translated by Lindsay Turner), *Blur*